CONFESSIONS

CONFESSIONS

Stories to Rock Your Soul

A Memoir

Nadine Condon

McCAA BOOKS • SANTA ROSA, CA

McCaa Books
684 Benicia Drive #50
Santa Rosa, CA 95409

First published in 2022 by McCaa Books,
an imprint of McCaa Publications.

Library of Congress Control Number: 2022903038
ISBN 978-1-7378683-3-0 Paperback

Printed in the United States of America
Set in Minion Pro
Book and cover design by Waights Taylor Jr.

www.mccaabooks.com

This Book is dedicated to Honey, Mark Parsons

Life is a highway, I want to ride it all night long.
If you're going my way, I want to drive it all night long.

Tom Cochrane

Contents

Introduction

A light coastal breeze caressed my damp, naked skin. I stood dripping on the cliffside deck, under the glare of a full moon. Waves crashed noisily on the rocks far below as I surveyed the nighttime Pacific. Men and women mingled casually unclothed behind me, dipping in and out of the steamy hot baths. Joints were passed offhandedly. The smell of rotten eggs mixed sinuously with cheap incense and weed smoke. The only lights were votives which sputtered occasionally in the rising mist. I reveled in how free I felt. The mores of my conservative upbringing had melted away.

I was in the fabled bohemian enclave of Big Sur. This was the Esalen Institute, that famous retreat center and breeding ground of the human potential movement. Esalen was a west coast mecca for radical new ways of thinking and counterculture interest.

It was 1971. I was a college student, originally from the South, camping with friends in the Big Sur redwoods. I had been roused from my sleeping bag at midnight by a local denizen, a friend of a friend. She had sensed my desire for deeper exploration of the California lifestyle. She hadn't woken up anyone else in my group. Only me. Locals living in Big Sur, then as now, would gather in the early morning hours to commune in these natural hot tubs. Long considered sacred waters by the Native population, they were usually reserved for paying guests of the Esalen Institute. I felt anointed into a secret club.

I had a transcendent moment of clarity there, peering out over the vastness of the ocean. The waters seemed to gleam with possibility. It was simple. I wanted to live like these people.

I knew right there and then, in a nanosecond, I would accomplish all this and more. The West Coast would beckon me until I gave in to her entreaties. There was a big life in front of me. I was completely positive about it. I've never, ever forgotten how I felt that exalted evening, and the sense of assuredness that enveloped me.

That's how it started for me, traipsing into a future I could feel but not see. I was the fortunate, youngest daughter of a lively Irish Catholic family of upward mobility. Everything came easily to me. Friends. School. Sports. With education, talent, and a bubbling wellspring of curiosity, I was ready to take on the world. I knew early on I wasn't going to follow the prescribed path my parents hoped for me. I had hopes and dreams that far exceeded my hometown. This was ground zero for me.

That pivotal visit to that sulfurous sanctuary of human possibility was a kiss of recognition from the otherworldly frisson of "knowingness." After a lifetime of wrestling with the enigma of this palpable energy force, I'm now comfortable calling these indelible moments of comprehension ones of *the Spirit*. You might call it the Divine. Higher Power. The Source. God. The Universe, The name doesn't matter. What does matter is acknowledgement of this sublime, supernal entity. It's that unerring insight-instinct-intuition that permeates our entire being—impossible to explain and beyond logic. It's that deep gut feeling when we just "know"—the right path, the right approach, the right action.

I've come to understand this Spirit as my one constant companion, offering guidance as I speed through my days. Once it warned me of grave danger, and I ignored it—to disastrous ends. On another occasion it led me to a Super Bowl ring. That same Spirit forced me to keep re-meeting my husband until I took off my blinders and finally saw him. Sometimes I listened to it and thrived. My music showcase festival Nadine's Wild Weekend comes to mind. Often, I just didn't understand and so bumbled around, running into the same obstacles over and over. I have had as many failures as successes, if not more. But Spirit has always been there, whispering, molding, cajoling.

These tales of my hedonistic, exciting Rock & Roll life; my unexpected journey into the hospice field as a late-life career; my wrenching stories of loss and service; and my zig-zag journey to and from faith, are meant to inspire. I know from my own rough and tumble history, as confusing and stressful as life was, change is possible. We can step through our fears. We can mature spiritually. We can become aware, responsible adults. Or not. It's not for me to judge anyone's path or choices.

These true-life stories reflect my peripatetic adventures, good and bad, and the knowledge (or lack thereof) that was the result of these experiences. You will see yourself in some of these stories. My personalized accounts represent universal, time-honored challenges. Who amongst us hasn't shied away from demanding situations, unwilling to listen to that small voice inside? Who else has been incapable of stepping through whatever forces hold us back? Who hasn't struggled with the God question? Whether you want to relive my wild Rock & Roll adventures vicariously, or glean greater insight into tangled yet more consequential matters, this book is for you.

PART ONE

California Dreaming

Ever after that eventful trip to Big Sur in college, my objective was always to live in northern California. I intentionally moved to Boston first, wanting an East Coast experience before I committed to the Golden State. I worked in the office of the *Boston After Dark* alternative weekly newspaper, which later became the *Boston Phoenix*. It was a hub for future superstar writers like Janet Maslin (*New York Times*). I spent time with new friends at Harvard's Lowell House or went clubbing to see the blues greats play live—Muddy Waters, T Bone Walker, Pinetop Perkins, Howlin' Wolf, Lightnin' Hopkins, Sonny Terry and Brownie McGhee, Hound Dog Taylor, John Lee Hooker, Jimmy Reed. Two years in Boston restored some of my confidence after a college ordeal. I intentionally buried the rest, impatient to move to the promised land of California. While Boston was a cool town, the west coast remained my dream.

Finally arriving in Berkeley at the tail end of 1974, I plunged into the counterculture fray, embracing experiences like others eat candy. I stuffed huge gobs of living into my days and nights. I was a bumper car, careening from encounter to encounter. I was like the Terminator, letting nothing derail me from my explorations. My curiosity was as broad as the Mississippi and as open as the plains I had left behind. My eye-witness account gives a glimpse into those golden days and all that followed...

1

San Francisco 1975

I moved west with college girlfriends, JK and ME. We spent six weeks touring America in our Dodge van before settling into a small boxy yellow house in the low-rent Berkeley flats. I lived in the converted garage, a barebones but roomy space. Barely catching our breath, we immediately made a beeline to the City. San Francisco in the mid-seventies was an irresistible smorgasbord of delights. It's impossible to overstate how wide-open the Bay Area was in those days. The Haight may have been dead, but the City was buzzing with every possibility imaginable. Gay, straight, up, down, sideways. San Francisco was a series of eclectic neighborhoods, each functioning as its own little village. You could start a conversation with a stranger on a Tuesday and end up three neighborhoods away by Thursday, without ever going home. I knew I was in the right place at the right time.

By the mid-70s, the Haight had fallen into gray, fog-shrouded despair. Populated by junkies and runaways there was little peace, love, and happiness there. Some desultory clubs still existed, and we mistook the ghosts of past bacchanals for current viability. We saw Bo Diddley and Lady Bo play a small club called the Cat's Cradle. After ninety minutes of Lady Bo and fifteen minutes of the great Bo, it was clear that the show, like the neighborhood, was living on past accolades.

I went to North Beach because I was a closet writer. I wanted to meet real Beat writers and drink from their souls of knowledge. The historical significance of the neighborhood was not lost on me. Jack Kerouac, Neal Cassidy, Allen Ginsberg, City Lights Bookstore, The Coffee Gallery (where Jorma Kaukonen had backed up Janis Joplin), The Hungry I (home of Bill Crosby; Mort Sahl; Lenny Bruce; Peter, Paul, and Mary). Alive or dead, these cultural muses called to me. This was my Paris of the '20s.

My most important discovery was the 1232 Saloon on Grant Avenue, the finest and oldest bar in San Francisco. We were greeted by an enormous, intricately carved wood back bar, filled with gleaming bottles of liquor. There was a long, matching front bar, and one large front window next to the entryway. It had a narrow, deep interior with a tiny stage in back for live music seven nights a week. The Saloon, then as now, was a drinking person's bar. No frilly drinks for them. Frequented by a lively mix of degenerates, poets, musicians, ne'er do wells, artists, motorcycle riders, drug dealers, street musicians, and counter-culture celebs, the Saloon embodied everything that was right with San Francisco. Everyone that entered the Saloon was on equal ground within its packed domain. I was drunk, both figuratively and literally, with the headiness of my bold move to San Francisco.

Within a few months, I had met more people in that venerable chapel of drinking, than in my entire two years in Boston. I even met a man who would later change my life in every way, at that hallowed bar. But there were other adventures to be had in that City by the Bay before Rock & Roll came into my life.

I toured the city wide and far outside the Saloon too, scooting around in my cheap, banged-up VW Karmann Ghia. The LGBT movement was in its infancy and San Francisco was the hub for gay men and women. The gay bars were shamelessly libertine, and new to me. My favorite was that cavernous space of flashing strobes and thunderous music, the Stud, on Folsom Street. Despite the clientele being overwhelmingly male homosexuals, I was always propositioned for sex in that melee of male testosterone, exposing the ever-shifting boundaries of our sexual mores at the time.

I also began playing billiards to meet people, haunting bars with pool tables throughout the Bay Area: iconic watering holes in the City like Gino and Carlo's and The Bus Stop. Neighborhood pubs like Maud's, a predominantly lesbian bar whose pool tables were covered in red felt, or Dick's, the only straight bar in the heavily gay Castro district. I motored up to the Russian River vacation area to shoot pool with ragtag river denizens. I drove to Marin County hippie haunts where Janis Joplin had shot pool, or Smitty's in Sausalito. I sauntered into these establishments ordering bourbon on the rocks while putting my quarter down on the table in what I hoped was a sexy challenge.

Not that I knew what sexy meant, beyond going braless. At that time, sex was simply a way to keep the conversation going. I slept with people because they intrigued me. It was part of the adventure. I was comfortably open with my body. I drove regularly to Muir Beach to sunbathe naked on the clothing-optional side. I even went topless while horseback riding bareback once in Tilden Park, Berkeley. It was a hot summer's day, and I took off my long sleeve top. The male hiker I encountered up in those dry, eucalyptus scented hills off Grizzly Peak Boulevard, was thrilled to see my version of Lady Godiva canter past him nonchalantly.

I worked selling stereos, quite a prestigious job for a girl. Later I bartended at a beer/wine joint in North Beach while collecting unemployment from the stereo job. Jobs had no meaning for me; they were simply a way to pay the rent. Instead of a career, life was full of all the encounters I had dreamed of having one day. I went to poetry readings, concerts, alternative news conferences, music clubs, drum circles, political rallies, and underground films. I met my life-long friend D when I applied for a job on a Berkeley underground weekly. The newspaper never got off the ground but I'm godmother to D's kids and their kids. I learned to balance the arm of a turntable while being tutored in the mores of gay club hopping by a fellow southerner, LD, who remained a pal until his recent passing.

We went to music all around the Bay, including dancing every Sunday night at the rowdy Longbranch Saloon in Berkeley. The Shakers, a young, white reggae band, had a spirited, loyal crowd of pulsating dancers. That's where I saw pre-fame rock star Eddie Money strut in, bedecked in fur, bravado, perfect rock hair, and an entourage. We followed the band Lisa and Debby, talented women playing rocking blues, underscoring our feminist fervor. Debby would be wailing on her guitar wearing a long granny dress while Lisa growled out blues. They played the first Hooker's Ball, a Halloween fundraiser for prostitutes organizing for wages and protection, held in the ballroom of the glitzy Hyatt Hotel downtown. A male attendee tied a whip to his penis, the handle and tail jutting out of his red bikini briefs, briefly scandalizing me, before we went back to dancing. We idolized Commander Cody and His Lost Planet Airmen, never missing a chance to see them play Texas swing-rockabilly-rock& roll at the capacious beer and wine joint, the Keystone Berkeley. And of course, we were bona fide Deadheads.

I saw pre-fame Patti Smith read poetry to a small crowd in a radical bookstore, her lank hair covering her face, the audience held rapt by the drama of her verse. I wrote feminist rants to TIME Magazine, and was a founding subscriber to Ms. Magazine, along with spending time in a female consciousness-raising group. I followed the Patty Hearst kidnapping avidly, even attending a forum on the kidnapping, improbably held at the swank Palace Hotel downtown, chaired by Patty's cousin Will Hearst. I took note of the local literati, including counter-culture journalist Paul Krassner (*The Realist*) who walked around with sheaves of papers falling out of his overstuffed notebooks. Later, in an underground coffee house, I met an ex-con who introduced me to his ex-con radical collective. Sitting in their sunny ghetto kitchen, I felt cutting edge. I had never felt more alive. It was a far cry from my old Kentucky home.

2

Lovers and Losers

I met so many striking characters in the San Francisco Bay Area that I felt like I was in a Dickens novel. The cast of originals and eccentrics was significant and never-ending. Here are a few seminal individuals and events burned into my memory. True to form, I met many of these folks in the iconic 1232 Saloon on Grant Avenue.

One of the first I met in North Beach was BJ, the blue-collar ex-roadie with biker connections. With a mop of unruly, curly hair and a grizzled countenance, he was bow-legged and stocky, a lengthy key chain permanently attached to his jeans. Lucky for me, after a brief tryst, he recognized my youthful naiveté and took it upon himself to watch out for us girls. He recognized the class difference immediately between his hard-scrabble background and our cultured girls school demeanor, even though we were trying hard to hide it. Gruff on the outside but a softie inside, BJ quickly morphed from brief lover to protective Big Daddy. I got a glimpse of the cracks in his life when we ran into his daughter on Haight Street. She was thirteen and nearly feral, supposedly living with her druggy Mom. I was surprised and saddened by the casual neglect that hung over her. Just another abandoned child from the Summer of Love.

BJ loved showing us how "connected" he was in the city and took us backstage to all the free concerts. We saw Hot Tuna at Stern Grove. Their vintage car, seen on a famous album cover, was parked backstage. We were thrilled to get close to the car, even more the band. Then there was the free Jefferson Starship concert in Golden Gate Park. BJ put us up on one side of the stage, where we boogied with the pros. We were enamored with Jefferson Starship and would regularly cruise by their mansion on Fulton Street, looking for their album-cover adorned equipment trucks.

To attend that same Jefferson Starship concert, my roommates JK, ME, and I had hitchhiked over from Berkeley. After the concert we were leaning against a parked BMW, with our thumbs out, waiting for a ride out of the park and down to the freeway entrance. We were astonished when David Freiberg, Jefferson Starship bassist/keyboardist, casually walked up and announced we were sitting on his car! He nonchalantly gave us a ride down to the freeway entrance, while we sat quietly, trying to emit vibes of coolness. We were unable to say a word, struck dumb with shyness in the presence of a real rock star. A scant four years later, I was working with this man and his band.

Another person I encountered was the underrated Beat poet, Jack Micheline, a short, barrel-chested man with bristly silver hair and a crusty, profane demeanor. His skin was rough and leathery. Jack was a brilliant artist, writing poetry and painting in an apartment over the Libertarian Bookstore. As were the times, we hooked up briefly. I'll never forget lying around naked, discussing writers. He must have thought I did not consider him as significant as his contemporaries. "But I AM a published writer," he yelled at me, jumping up to grab one of his slender books of poetry, opening it to read aloud. "I'm not just some jack-off," he hissed menacingly. I'll never forget that brief glimpse into his deep, roiling anger at the fickleness of acclaim. Later Jack painted more, but he never received the credit due him, until after he died, twenty-five years after our trysts. They found him slumped dead, at the end of the BART rapid transit line, in a distant suburb, far from his San Francisco home.

One of the most interesting men I had the pleasure of meeting was C. I was intrigued by the long, gray braid which fell halfway down his back. A tall, older man, C had twinkling eyes and a knowing smile. I came to find he was an avowed sensualist. Taking me to his house was my first surprise. It was down an alley of aging Victorian flats in an unfashionable neighborhood south of Market Street. Entering the house on Minna Street, you walked up steep, tight stairs lined with a sizable collection of severed dolls' heads. Reaching the top step, I cautiously looked around. Paintings, colorful strands of beads, dramatic scarves, richly embroidered cushions, tassled lamps, stacks of books, velvet chairs, sculptures, and framed photos adorned the living room. There was not an inch of uncluttered surface in view. And the wildest assortment of artsy accoutrements I'd ever seen. (Mayan carved stone dildoes anyone?) It felt breathtakingly exotic.

If I thought that was an experience, it was nothing compared to the next morning when his strikingly beautiful Russian-born wife swept into the bedroom offering juice and a gracious good morning to us. Turbaned, scarved, bejeweled, and perfectly made-up, M was non-plussed finding me with her older husband. They lived unconventionally and this was not her concern.

C was a photographer with a sharp eye. He had a special affinity for finding the perfect light. M taught traditional Eastern dance, as well as buying and selling collectibles gleaned from flea markets. She was just beginning her nascent jewelry design, for which she is now renowned. Buckminster Fuller was godfather to one of their daughters. They hosted soirees every Wednesday night, with dancers, artists, and Bohemians. I was smitten with their scene.

Although I ceased sleeping with C, uncomfortable with the arrangement, thankfully that did not diminish our friendship. I started going out with them on their adventures around the Bay Area. C would drive us in their ancient Rolls Royce, which had the English right-sided steering wheel. He would be alone in the front as the chauffeur, while we, the female acolytes, would be ensconced in the back with M, like traveling dignitaries. We would be dressed in feathers, scarves, and other outré finery, carrying drinks and food, with items of saleable interest jammed among us in the enormous backseat as we sailed across bridges. We would haunt the flea markets or drive up to Juanita's restaurant in the wine country for lunch. I was giddy with being accepted into their sophisticated, avant-garde world. They became unwitting, valuable tutors in the art of living outside cultural boundaries.

I'm neglecting scores of other folks I met. Like the easy-going, balding blond-haired person who lived in the Haight and turned me onto my first sex toy; the smiling cable car brakeman who attempted to cajole me into a threesome; the motorcycle-riding Canadian with the speedy Yamaha racing bike. A few Berkeleyites would wander in too, like the UC Berkeley graduate student who was taking a master class from Joan Didion. He would breathlessly relate her halting, nervous teaching style of wrapping and unwrapping a rubber band around her wrist incessantly, while I listened raptly. There was dark, brooding Billy Roberts, writer of the Jimi Hendrix anthem "Hey Joe," prowling North Beach between publishing checks. Amongst all this meeting and drinking, smoking, and doping, Bob Kaufmann, the Beat poet who was revered in France and penniless here at home, would wander up and down Grant Avenue ranting and raving. Just another day in paradise at the Saloon.

Yet, under these rosy memories lay the unspoken stories we rarely let see the light of day. Birth control snafus. Money issues. My continuing night fears of shadowy, empty streets left my heart racing. Walking the four blocks from the bus stop to our little cracker box home at night was an exercise in sheer determination, before I scraped together $400 to buy my beat-up Ghia.

There were plenty of losers along the way too. The handsome troubadour who besotted me until I found out he had a bleeding head of lice; the rude drug dealer with the vintage Mercedes, the curly-locked redhead I picked up hitching, who took my extra Stones ticket; that ill-advised drive home from Bolinas in the wee hours, which found me trapped in a roadside ditch overnight; the Bad Boy lover I adored, who betrayed me, sleeping with MA, the beautiful writer with the smart mouth. (MA later became a life-long friend).

These rummies fell through the cracks because none of us knew how to set boundaries. Nor could we discern the good from the bad and the ugly. We were coddled, cherished daughters of affluence. Our family lives had been prescribed and structured. We had little insight in judging human beings. Long-hair plus an affinity for drinking and drugs were our inadequate, dubious youthful criteria. A few inappropriate folks traipsed across the threshold until we got more proficient at recognizing members of our tribe who had similar values.

Our myopic blunders led to some shameful experiences. Others were hurtful. We are all capable of doing terrible things in any decade of our lives, but the twenties seem especially fraught with unruly behavior. Yet, I reveled in living life with no regrets. You took your lumps and went back out the door.

It was part of living a manly life, full throttle. By the time I hit thirty, I had the emotional scars and bruises I'd have if I'd gone ten rounds with Muhammad Ali. This didn't stop me from barreling forward like a barely controlled freight train.

But first there was Nick the Greek.

3

Nick the Greek

It was also against the backdrop of the Saloon that I met musician Nick Gravenites. I hadn't really known of Nick before entering the territory of the Saloon. But within that dim, dank domain, he was somewhat of a legend. A first-generation Greek from South Side Chicago, he had been a tough, juvenile-delinquent kid. He was saved from total ruin by his remarkable intelligence. Hanging out at the blues bars around the University of Chicago, Nick met other disenfranchised white boys like himself who worshiped the electric blues heard in those clubs. This wasn't sweet harmonic folk singing. This was raunchy, gritty blues distilled by years of hard luck and trouble. These boys tried to emulate their black blues heroes, finally getting proficient enough to play the blues circuit in Chicago, an unheard-of achievement. The Paul Butterfield Blues Band was different. They were the first integrated blues band. Their mojo, the ability to grasp the essence of blues playing, won them a legion of black and white fans. Muddy Waters, the great blues master and kingpin of the genre, took them under his wing, not unlike a father would his sons.

Nick went back and forth from Chicago to San Francisco, finally relocating in SF for good in the '60s. He brought all the sensibilities of electric blues with him to his new friends in the Bay Area---Quicksilver Messenger Service, Janis Joplin, Big Brother, and the like. These new musicians were yearning to go electric, tired of the constraints of acoustic music. All over the world young players were experimenting with the new electric sounds derived from black rhythm and blues (the Beatles, the Rolling Stones, The Yardbirds). Soon Bob Dylan would shock Newport Jazz Festival by going electric, backed by this same Paul Butterfield Blues Band.

Nick was in the middle of this cultural-musical maelstrom, influencing musicians in a behind-the-scenes manner that has never been adequately appreciated. Nick wrote Butterfield's first masterpiece "Born in Chicago." Both Nick and his first wife became Janis Joplin's friends and confidants. Nick helped Janis put her Kozmic Blues band together, while taking her place as singer in Big Brother after Janis left that band. He produced Quicksilver Messenger Service's first album and was a founding member of the band Electric Flag, one of the first rock bands to incorporate horns. He produced Brewer and Shipley's "One Toke Over the Line Sweet Jesus" and wrote songs covered by Pure Prairie League and Tracy Nelson.

Nick made a goodly amount of money from the last Janis Joplin record album, *Pearl*. Janis was to go into the studio the next day to record a song Nick had written just for her, "Buried Alive in the Blues." Janis accidentally overdosed on heroin that night, alone in her hotel room, needle still in her arm. With her unexpected death, the record sold millions and Nick's song, having been completed in the studio with all the tracks except Janis' vocal rendition, was included as the last song on the record, a fitting coda to her brief, bright life.

With his Janis money, Nick bought a house in Mill Valley, California, and a brand-new Mercedes Benz. He semi-retired to a life of leisurely pursuits, occasionally writing and playing music according to whim. He adopted the role of consigliere for his musician friends, as they all settled into life post '60s.

This was Nick's life when I met him in 1975. The dope smoking juvie from the rough southside of Chicago had turned into the hip, country squire of music. With that kind of resume, he was irresistible to me.

I was also a Janis Joplin acolyte. It's an understatement to I say I worshiped at the church of Janis. The roar of passion that came out of her mouth captured me from its first notes. She channeled Ike and Tina, Otis Redding and James Brown with soul shaking, soul rumbling music. I wanted to be like her, a *woman* among men. I patterned much of my persona on hers. I was the equal of any man. I was hard drinking and hard loving. I donned purple glasses and wore my hair long and natural. Seeing her in person in 1969 was one of the highlights of my young, suburban life.

I was intoxicated with the possibility of talking with a man who had known Janis. I watched timorously but yearningly while Nick drank and bantered with the locals in the Saloon. Soon enough we found ourselves in the empty bar on the same afternoon. We started talking casually and hit it off right away. Nick was a soulful, cranky man with a fierce intellect. His was a gruff, moody persona, with a dazzling mind and a hearty laugh. He was also a bit impenetrable. Nick loved an audience who appreciated his past exploits, and I was an eager audience. Sitting with Nick on those ancient bar stools, listening to his escapades with his famous friends, was the best music education I could ever receive.

Nick saw something in me that I did not see in myself. When I met him, I was "Mimi" to everyone. "Mimi" was my childhood nickname for Mary, as in Mary Nadine, my legal name, and it had naturally stuck into adulthood. Nadine was my mother's name, and it was not a name you wanted growing up. Too old fashioned. Nick didn't think the name "Mimi" suited me. One day in the Saloon, he asked me what it stood for. When I told him he immediately seized on my middle name of Nadine and told me that was a "Rock & Roll name." From that moment on, Nick only called me Nadine. I was flushed by this attention. I had a special name (albeit my own name) bestowed on me by someone who had been one of the architects of the music revolution. Life was thrilling.

4

Lurching Through Hawaii

Nick was married and I had various beaus when we met. It was the times. We developed a friendship beyond our occasional trysts. Against this backdrop of random assignations, while playing pool at the Paradise Café bar in San Francisco, I fell madly and unexpectedly in love with a handsome man who dubbed himself "Bad Boy Billy." He was an Ivy League graduate, a sailor from Rhode Island. I've always fallen for smart men. I was head over heels, this being my first significant adult relationship post high-school love. After months of dating, I committed to Bad Boy Billy, so Nick was relegated to friend status. Unfortunately, I discovered rather late in the game that Bad Boy Billy was a serial philanderer. Despite my having this hurtful knowledge about his womanizing, his betrayal came to full light as we were in the process of moving to Hawaii to make our fortunes. Despite my conflicted emotions, I felt trapped into following through with our plans.

Our so-called strategy to get rich unraveled like a dollar-store rug as soon as we landed on the Islands. We flew to the sleepy, undeveloped Big Island. Unlike touristy Maui, the island of Hawaii was like a foreign country. It had few resorts, odd food, and everyone spoke pidgin English. We stayed with a casual friend from North Beach. Unfortunately, our shaky blueprint for getting rich in Hawaii was based on this person's faulty information, putting us in the hole quickly. No one

30

was interested in buying the LSD we thought would fund this adventure. Adding insult to injury, the cannabis farming we hoped to start was controlled by a small, secret club we could not penetrate.

To correct our course, we bought a 1965 Dodge Dart from a sleepy-eyed Samoan in the busy parking lot of the Hilo, Hawaii Safeway. We quickly christened the car Lurch. Lurch had red leather seats and enough rust to camouflage the paint. His chrome wasn't bad either. After shipping him to Maui on a barge, we followed, hoping to find restaurant work in the booming resorts of Kaanapali.

Although we both found work on Maui, he as a waiter and me as a hostess at a swanky beach club, we couldn't seem to find purchase in this ill-begotten adventure. Between staying with strangers, being broke, and lingering distrust and anger on my part, our frustrations mounted. Our disenchantment culminated in a knock-down-drag-out argument at the Lahaina marina. We were screaming at one another. The friends we had been staying with had returned to the mainland abruptly, leaving us high and dry. We had no money and no prospect of a place to sleep that night. Bad Boy Billy was acting cavalier about this dreadful situation.

Our furious words flew through the balmy air, disappointment rife between us. I could hear the sailboat lanyards clanking against the masts as we stood on the wharf. The boozed-up piano player at the Pioneer Inn was playing a rollicking keyboard medley, but the music fell flat against my anger. The warm Pacific water lapped peacefully against the stone breakwater while Bad Boy and I glared at each other. We had moved to Hawaii looking for high-flying adventure. That high-flying life was currently crashing against the rocks as we stood there tensely. We looked into each other's eyes accusatorily, each blaming the other. I was semi-hysterical, my confidence in tatters. Bad Boy feigned nonchalance, but I could see worry in his dark, bloodshot eyes.

Eventually, we climbed into trusty old Lurch, and drove silently out of town. Bad Boy Billy was now actually remorseful our escapade had taken such a poor turn. I was simply mad and scared. A short way out of town, there was a cane field that hid an old Chinese cemetery. We nosed Lurch down a dusty road of red dirt. Driving through tall, sticky stems we parked in a mostly concealed spot, deep within the tract. I was terrified a local Hawaiian gang would find and accost us, since haoles (non-Islanders) were bitterly resented at the time.

It was miserable. Even with all the windows rolled down, the humidity was suffocating and the mosquitoes gigantic. The heralded Hawaiian ocean breezes could not penetrate inland. I laid there anxious, sweaty, sticky, and riddled with insect bites, while my hopes crashed and burned. Sleepless in the back seat of that junky car, I wondered what had happened to my semi-charmed life; it lay buried under those shattered pipe dreams. The entire adventure had been a dismal, soul crushing experience.

Bad Boy Billy and I never got back on track. Our poor luck continued, touching every aspect of our relationship. Months later, after almost coming to blows in an alcohol-fueled dustup, I called it quits and flew back to the Bay Area. Several years later Bad Boy Billy showed up again. We very briefly reconciled before bad behavior caused us to crash and burn for the final time. What can I say: sometimes I'm just a slow learner.

Thirty years later, friends informed me he was dying in a distant state. I wrote him a goodbye note. As I sealed the envelope for mailing, a jolt of electricity shot through my body. I knew then we were both finally at peace with our past.

5

I'm a Music Manager

While I had been off on my half-baked Hawaiian scheme, Nick's life was going through its own upheavals. He and his second wife divorced. After returning to the Bay Area from Hawaii to lick my wounds, I showed up at one of Nick's gigs, unannounced. We were thrilled to see one another. I spent my first ever night in his actual house that evening, post-show. One night turned into two, then into three, and onward. We reveled in being together. Soon he invited me to move in with him. I relocated to his Mill Valley A-frame perched on the hillside high in the trees and began a new chapter in my Bay Area sojourn. It was a sweet time for the two of us, free to show our loving emotions and have adventures together in beautiful Marin County, north of San Francisco.

I was now officially "Nadine," ditching my Mimi nickname. I longed to get into the music business but was uncharacteristically shy in taking the first step. I chafed in the role of musician's girlfriend. It was too dismissive for me. At this same time, Nick wanted to revive his career and start performing more regularly. And that's how my lengthy career in the music business began. Out of necessity. Organically. Nick needed a manager, and I needed an opportunity to jump into a music business career. I now had a legitimate reason to be in the business and develop my own talents. It was perfect synchronicity, and we made a good team.

Nick, bridging the creative gap between blues and psychedelia, was an irreplaceable introduction to the scene. Nick knew the intricacies of the business better than most musicians, having been managed himself by the legendary rock manager Albert Grossman. He passed his knowledge on to me, the neophyte. Nick knew all the members of the Band and we would hang out with them at their hotel when they were in San Francisco. I would spend hours talking on the phone in the wee hours to the inebriated harmonica ace Paul Butterfield, Nick's oldest friend. Sultry singer Maria Muldaur, the eccentric guitarist John Cippollina, Brewer and Shipley, and blues great James Cotton were a few of the musicians I had the honor of meeting. Extremely talented bassist/keyboardist Pete Sears (Jefferson Starship, Rod Stewart, Moonalice) and his wife Jeannette (also a songwriter) became very dear friends.

Still in my twenties, I flourished in my management roll, writing press releases, booking live shows, paying musicians, arranging for the band's live performance needs. I loved being in the center of the musical mix. Creativity could be found everywhere you looked. The Bay Area was flourishing with second and third wave musical heroes in the making. I would pay Huey Lewis $10 to sit in and play harmonica at shows with Nick, before he started Huey Lewis and the News. Same story with James "Toast" Ralston, a superb guitar player, before he went on to tour with Tina Turner for the next thirty years. My generation's talents were unfurling, and I wanted to join those ranks. Like every other twenty-something from time immemorial, I wanted more. I was hungry for the proverbial big-time.

That siren call became an insistent wail after Nick followed the Clash onstage at a feebly- organized outdoor pop festival. Chet Helm's Tribal Stomp at the old Monterey Fairgrounds (home of the original Monterey Pop) featured the old guard (like Nick and company) with the new sound (like the Clash, one of which, the drummer Topper Headon, had puked onstage right before we came on). It was a chaotic scene, one that found me wandering around in a mini dress, wielding a fifth of brandy with my usual aplomb, trying to stand out.

I was tired of dealing with local club owners and yearned for a national stage. My feelings solidified as my personal relationship with Nick started to crumble. We both started to make plans for futures that didn't include the other, though we remained respectful friends. I lobbied bass/keyboardist Pete Sears and his wife Jeannette for their help in getting me a job with Pete's band, the legendary Jefferson Starship. We were close friends and had raucous nights of poker at each other's houses.

Luckily, it wasn't long before the next murky chapters came into view. The Jefferson Starship hired me as a publicist, and I began my new job in October 1979, the same day their new single "Jane" was released. The 80s were right around the corner and I was chomping at the bit to make a mark, any kind of mark, on the San Francisco scene.

PART TWO

The Rock Years

Rock & Roll music defined my generation. The 1970s doubled down on this cultural phenomenon called Rock & Roll. Many of us, myself included, dreamed of collaborating with our generational heroes. We got the opportunity with the explosion of rock bands appearing on the scene, the expansion of record labels, the burgeoning number of record stores and the proliferation of FM radio stations. The business of managing, promoting, and selling artists stepped out of the realm of Mom and Pop and became big business. Many of us found unexpected careers in this hotpot of musical confluences. I was drawn to the brilliance of the "San Francisco Sound." In time, my San Francisco music heroes became colleagues, trusted friends, and dear family. Through my work with Jefferson Starship, later simply Starship, I was able to make an independent name for myself in the music industry. I maintained a credible independent music business, promoting, managing, and producing for nearly thirty years. My career culminated in a multi-day music showcase festival, a music business seminar, and a "how-to" book for musicians. These vignettes of my adventures in Rock & Roll show how that scene shaped my future…

6

First Big-Time Rock & Roll Trip

There I was, mid- November 1979, winging my way east to join up with the legendary San Francisco band, Jefferson Starship. My first road trip with this band truly cemented my obsession with everything "music business."

Through my connection with bassist Pete Sears and his songwriting wife, Jeannette Sears, I landed in the perfect position as a publicist with the Jefferson Starship. The Jefferson Starship organization was a successful, respected, professional outfit. Successful through two decades, the band was embarking on yet a third decade, high on the charts, with another smash single and a highly anticipated national tour. This was the band that had put the San Francisco psychedelic sound into the consciousness of the world. This was rock royalty, not one of the reunion bands you see now, playing your local casino. Rock & Roll was still years away from being diluted by MTV, American Idol, and video games. Rock bands were those brightly plumed, exotic birds that lived, played, breathed, dressed, related, heck, even screwed by a different code. Rock & Roll was the most exclusive club in the world, and I was winging my way east to join the founding members of this club. Heady stuff.

Because this celebrated group demanded VIP treatment, I enjoyed the same benefits in management as the band. What dichotomy my life was then. I parked my little rusted-out VW wagon at the airport and boarded a wide-bodied jet from San

Francisco to Chicago. It was the first time I had flown in the pampered, inordinately expensive first-class section (no mileage upgrades back then, passengers/companies paid for those seats). I ate and drank my way across the country in a state of enthralling comfort. Upon landing I was met by a shiny black limousine, complete with driver in cap and gloves and ferried to the fancy Water Tower hotel downtown. Impressed concierge staff escorted me to my expansive room on the 32nd floor. It had a sweeping view of Chicago's famous Gold Coast, the plushest towels I'd ever seen in my life and a gigantic bed. I couldn't believe this was my life.

After delivering the ounce of coke I had casually carried in my luggage, I attended my first Jefferson Starship concert as a member of the management office. When I got to the hall, our crew was busy setting up for the show. One of the crew, not knowing I was the new publicist, but watching me for a while before the concert started, came over and asked if I was the band's hostess. I haughtily informed him that I was the new publicist, which conveyed not only a certain mark of distinction but authentic business legitimacy. After that, everyone treated me with a bit more deference. I was in "management," meaning I traveled with the band and was treated like the band. They were "crew," traveled like a crew, bunked in cheap hotels and busses, and treated like crew, generally at the band's beck and call.

Despite this initial *faux pas*, however, these silly class distinctions quickly fell by the wayside. Because of the constant travel, a Rock & Roll band on the road is its own insulated universe. And everyone, band, crew, and management, is dependent symbiotically on everyone else. Or at least it was this way for Jefferson Starship. Later, touring with the Who under vastly different circumstances, I had a young singer opening for that band, Ryan Downe, I found the class system we disdained in American Rock & Roll to be alive and well with the English. Despite my rock credentials, I was treated like crap. As I toured with Jefferson Starship through the decade, people became my family, lovers, friends, protectors, and *compadres*. On this first night though, all I saw were hunky guys running about setting up for the show and asking me if I needed anything. I basked in the attention.

I elicited strong amount of interest as the "new girl." At close to six feet tall, I'm sure I stood out. I do have presence. I was dressed in my official working-for-a-rock-band attire. One of the most stylish rock wives to ever inhabit the scene, generous Jeannette Sears, had graciously helped with my outfit. High heels, low cut silk blouse that tied in front, long swirling skirt cut high in front---nothing mainstream. My mother called these, "*my costumes*." But there was an unspoken understanding that I had the image of the band to uphold in my official position. I needed to look coolly hip yet professional. I was sure my outfit struck just the right chord.

This first concert was a revelation. For the first time, I stood directly off stage, just feet from the performers. I was free to wander around behind stage and in the dressing rooms. There was no area off-limits to me. I quickly found the best observation spot to be at the monitor mixer. There were large road cases for equipment that I could sit on to watch the show while drinking a cold beer out of the band's backstage stash. The infamous LSD genius Owsley (also known as "Bear") was staffing the onstage monitors sound board. He had long been associated with San Francisco bands and Ken Kesey's LSD loving Merry Pranksters. Relationships notwithstanding, he sometimes fell asleep while manning the sound controls during the show. No one seemed to get upset or even notice, except me.

After the show, an announcement was made that the "other" San Francisco band, the Grateful Dead, was playing across town and we were all invited. Because I was a Deadhead at the time, I excitedly raced to get into one of the limos. My friends weren't going to believe I was not only working for Jefferson Starship, but then going to see the Dead that same night! I was the only one who got into the car to go to the show. No one else had the slightest interest. Talk about a busman's holiday! The driver drove cross-town. When I showed up at the stage door with my Jefferson Starship staff laminated pass, I was greeted like an old friend and basically given the run of the backstage. I didn't know a soul, but it didn't matter. Later, someone came and stood on the side of the stage with me. It was "Bear." I guess he woke up. When I was ready to go, the limo, the driver having patiently waited for me, the lowly publicist, costing the record company hundreds of dollars per hour, took me back to my hotel. My head was spinning with all the sights, sounds and power of the evening.

The next night the record label took all of us out to dinner at one of the trendiest restaurants in town. We drank bottles and bottles of Dom Perignon champagne to toast the release of the new album *Freedom at Point Zero*. Bottles were opened with abandon, a glass or two poured, a sip taken (or not), and then forgotten. I remember going from table to table picking up half-full bottles in wonderment of the sheer excessive waste, thinking I should do something about it. What, save the half-drunk bottles for another time? My eyes were as big as saucers. It was a giddy evening, complete with a noticeably young Jon Pareles from *Rolling Stone* magazine, who was sent out to do a story on the third Jefferson Starship reincarnation. Mr. Pareles is now the *New York Times* rock critic.

Two days later we moved to Milwaukee for the next gig. I had quickly gotten into the rhythm of the road: drinking and doing drugs after the show with the gang. I had not yet had sex on the road only because everything was moving too fast. We played for a promoter in Milwaukee who was famous for providing gorgeous ladies for the bands who came to town. As a member of the management staff, the promoter wanted to take care of me too. At the hotel bar, which is where I found you always congregated after a show, two good looking guys who worked for the promoter took me to a secluded area. They gave me line after line of cocaine. Anything I wanted, they were willing to do for me. In my naivete, I remember just not comprehending the situation.

Later in my career, I came to have a different response when promoter reps asked me what I needed. By then I was used to having everyone follow my orders. Florida was particularly memorable. There, when the rep asked me if he could do anything for me, I half kiddingly replied that he could get on his knees and take care of business. So, he did, lifting my skirt, right there while we were alone in the dressing room. Now that was service! But that future, was still ahead of me.

Later that same night in Milwaukee, we were in a band member's hotel room. It was 3:30 in the morning. In a few hours I was catching a commuter plane home to join my family in Louisville for Thanksgiving. It was the normal scene with band members, staff, crew, and label reps partying down. I was in deep discussion with one of the label reps and holding yet another fresh beer. I'll never forget him looking at me in amazement as he realized I was a normal, bright-eyed twenty-something like himself. Once again, someone saw some capability in me I didn't yet see in myself. The look on his face was incredulous, as he asked "What, my sweet Irish lassie, are you doing working for a rock band? You have so much on the ball, smart girl…"

Two hours later, having gotten no sleep, my mind a whirlwind of the sights and sounds of the prior few days, I wondered the same thing. I settled back in my seat on the little commuter plane for the ride home to Kentucky for Thanksgiving, in absolute wired exhaustion. It was the first, but not the last time, I would arrive home sleepless and bedraggled from the Rock & Roll road. My big-time music biz career had begun.

7

Super Bowl in Tampa

Many people attend sporting events but few get a *behind the curtain* view of the experience. For me, 1984 started out with a sports-drenched, once-in-a lifetime adventure when I was invited to go to the Super Bowl in Tampa, Florida with the Oakland Raiders. They were playing the Washington Redskins in the title game on January 22. I was friends with Mark Davis, whose Dad owned the Raiders. Mark was a bona fide music buff and was often at the same local shows I attended. Mark loved Rock & Roll, especially guitar players, and he was a big fan of our Jefferson Starship guitar player Craig Chaquico. We become like brother and sister.

It made sense. I was no longer a newcomer in the music business but a seasoned pro. I worked in a historically male profession and was "one of the guys." It didn't hurt that I was a huge sports fan and could spout stats with the best of them. And then there was the fact that when the Raiders moved to Los Angeles, I had introduced Mark to my music business friends in Los Angeles. From day one he was treated like royalty in Los Angeles.

I met Mark through my friend SF who was managing an iconic rock club in San Francisco called the Old Waldorf. SF had been on the ground floor at the birth of the modern music business and was friends with many of the music folks in LA. We were all one big happy family. Rock & Roll or football, it was all the same. That special camaraderie that comes from producing high value entertainment for the public connected us.

The Raiders marched through an improbable 1983 winning season with All-Pro Howie Long, former Heisman quarterback Jim Plunkett, former Heisman Trophy winner Marcus Allen and speedy wide-receiver Clifford Branch (who should be a Hall of Famer with those other Raiders.) When they advanced to the Super Bowl at Tampa Stadium, we were ecstatic. And when the call from Mark came inviting SF and me to join him and the team for the trip, we were over the moon. The air travel, hotels, transportation, game tickets were on the Raiders. Mark was always generous like that.

SF and I flew to LA brimming with excitement. We could probably have run faster than the plane flew in our eagerness to get to Tampa. Immediate to our landing the chaos, excitement and anticipation of the week hit home. The logistics were staggering for the Raiders staff and they did a fantastic job. The plane was met by their representatives who handed us information packets: hotel info, transport info, schedules, badges and tickets for everyone. After retrieving our bags, we were assigned shuttle vans to our different hotels. The great Hall of Famer Fred Bilitnekoff sat across from me on the ride to the hotel. I was too overcome to even speak to him. Me, who could walk up to any Hell's Angel or psychotic fan and command them to do what I told them to do, was intimidated in the presence of what I considered true sports greatness.

The madness that defines the Super Bowl came early when our shuttle took us to the host hotel for the Washington Redskins by mistake. There we were, Raiders family, friends, and former Raider greats, decked out in Raider swag. A throbbing mass of silver and black, we walked into the lobby, and ran smack into Redskin quarterback Joe Theisman, strolling through with a huge entourage of press and fans. Time seemed to slow down. You could feel the intensity in the air as some sort of primordial male combustion threatened to erupt. We were quickly hustled out of there before a fight could break out, loaded back on the shuttle and taken to the right accommodations. Our hotel was a faceless '60s-type motel not far from the Stadium, but we didn't care. If it was good enough for Freddy B., it was certainly good enough for us.

Later that day, we met up with friends and started partying. Our LA rock friends were staying across the Bay. It was a wild crew consisting of MTV chiefs, radio promo guys, and various rock managers. We taxied over to their digs where I ended up playing poker all night "with the big dogs." I crashed about 8:00 am in the living room of their suite and staggered back to Tampa late that day only to meet up with yet more friends. I disappeared with them for the night, leaving poor SF to deal with an infestation of ants in our room, coupled with a water leak. While I was out carousing, she was trying to move our room, with the help of a kindly security guard (no bell boys at this low rent joint). Unfortunately this move was complicated by the Rock & Roll paraphernalia and party favors we had thrown into the bedside nightstands. When I finally rolled in the next morning I was nonplussed about her travails.

On the actual day of Super Bowl XVIII, I was running on pure adrenalin. SF wore her Bobby Chandler jersey and I wore her John Matuzak jersey. The entire motel boarded the bus and we got to the stadium two hours before game time. Even arriving that early, the stadium was teeming. At that time, Tampa stadium was an old-school affair, with bleacher seats, no boxes and few amenities. We were sitting in the midst of Raider family nation, squeezed together like sardines, old, young, professionals, families, kids, scouts, football greats. I savored the moment with satisfaction and wished my Dad, who had died the previous summer, could see me.

SF and I had received silver and black pompons which we were madly shaking at any announcement, much to the chagrin of the elderly scout and his wife seated below us. Between my constant jumping up and down from my bleacher seat, my wild waving of the plastic fringe, and my bullhorn voice in a constant scream throughout the game, I'm sure I made their Super Bowl experience miserable. What did I care? I was living so large in my life I was oblivious to everything else. Later, getting beers, we ran smack dab into John Matuzak coming up the ramp. And there I was wearing his jersey! We both stopped dead in our tracks and eyeballed each other. He was a big guy, but I was no slouch in that department. He nodded. I nodded. We both moved on. It was a surreal moment.

The game was fantastic. The Raiders dominated the Redskins in every way. Cliff Branch scored in the first quarter and there was no looking back. Marcus Allen had a spectacular game and was named Super Bowl MVP. Our entire section was delirious with joy, tears, happiness, and vindication—the Raiders had moved from Oakland to L.A. and were reviled by many, including Pete Rozelle, then head of the NFL. Plus, the Redskins had been heavily favored. Weary with happiness, we boarded the buses back to our motels to change for the big victory party Mr. Davis was hosting. We couldn't have been happier for Mark and his Mom and Dad. They deserved this.

Refreshed and revived by showers ands fresh clothes, we walked into the victory party floating on air. We had WON! The giant ballroom was packed. Music was blaring. Giant crab claws, monster shrimp, and filet mignon skewers sat on tables groaning with luxurious food. Attending were players, families, kids, grandmothers, former greats, Mark's friends, our friends, hangers-on, has-beens, Raiderettes, other athletes, sportscasters, agents and politicians. It was a melting pot of American life circa 1984 as only Al Davis could construct. Mr. and Mrs. Davis, and Mark (this was the first we had seen him all week) graciously greeted all their guests, from the towel boys to the Governor. After a few laps around this penultimate cocktail party, we moved to a few of the player's suites upstairs, where they were holding private parties. We finally returned to our rooms in total, complete, utter exhaustion.

Which is why the departure call the next morning was particularly brutal. Dragging and bleary-eyed, we were herded together, and returned to the airport where all of us, players, coaches, staff, families and friends, waited to board an even bigger plane than the one we'd flown into Tampa. The depth of my exhaustion made rubbing shoulders with the Super Bowl champion players almost too much for me to appreciate. But three incidents remain vivid to this day.

The first episode is the incomparable Marcus Allen. Upon arrival at the airport, we were sent to a cordoned off private section to await our boarding. Marcus Allen, Super Bowl MVP came strolling down the airport corridor exuding star power. It literally radiated from his aura. He vibrated with rock star energy. As he sauntered along you realized how supremely confident he was in his own skin. Even after being around rock stars all my life, I've only seen that kind of power a few times--- Grace Slick had it in spades, along with Leon Russell.

The second memory is watching beefy defensive player Lyle Alzado playing with his angelic young son Justin, who looked about two or three years old at the time. This little boy, with his cherubic ringlets and huge uncomplicated smile of happiness, melted the human bulldozer who had flattened

49

opponents all season. Watching the vulnerability he displayed with his son, in juxtaposition with his on-field demeanor, was riveting. I witnessed this intimate moment silently, with something close to reverence.

My absolute best memory of this entire trip, however, came after we landed. Since we were a private flight, we landed in a non-commercial area of Los Angeles International airport. Stairs were brought to the plane so we could disembark. We descended to the tarmac and waited for the luggage to be unloaded. We continued waiting for quite some time, everyone hung over, tired, crabby, dirty, hot, sweaty, hungry…everyone just wanting to get home. Finally it became apparent that there had been some sort of miscommunication with the baggage handlers and they would not be arriving to unload our cargo.

So, how did we get our bags? The Raider football team, exhausted from a long season, and a longer night spent celebrating, these newly minted world champions of a game broadcast around the world, members of the most exclusive club in all of professional sports, formed two lines and started passing bags out of the hold, man by man, hand by hand, until all 300 of us had claimed our bags. Watching these worn out heroes unload our stinky, smelly, heavy bags with no ego, no hissy fits, no meltdowns, and with uncomplaining graciousness…well, for me, that picture will always and forever define the Raiders. Pure class. True champions. Raaaaaaaiderrrrrrrrrrs!

8

MTV Awards in NYC

I was standing at the side of the stage watching Madonna dance around in her little white wedding dress, showing her garters and shocking the world. It was 1984 and the very first MTV music awards, loosely patterned on the Grammy awards, but for videos, not songs. Although MTV has now morphed into reality shows, at that time it was a radical new medium for current popular music. MTV was the *TikTok* of its time and wildly successful channel. Everyone, the hippest of the hip, wanted to be on the awards show. Madonna was a desperate singer in danger of being written off as a passing fad with one dimensional talent. This event was her big break.

There I was, standing in the wings and watching the show with ho-hum interest. I was no longer wide-eyed but a hardened road warrior. I really did not care much about Madonna, or any of the other performers, for that matter. I was much more interested in all the behind-the-scenes action. What powerful business folks were hunkered down with their artists in those little dressing rooms and who had party favors? I spent all my time running around the labyrinth of backstage cubicles, cadging lines of cocaine, and grabbing beers. I was laughing, flirting, drinking, making new friends in the business while maintaining old ones, at the same time conducting business shop talk. You know, the usual.

I had the run of the backstage because our two lead singers, Grace Slick and Mickey Thomas were presenting awards. Also, Jefferson Starship had just weeks earlier played this legendary art deco venue, Radio City Music Hall, and all the facility crew knew me from our gig. When Jefferson Starship played, everybody wanted to come backstage. After so many years on top with icon status, the band had legions of friends and hangers-on. Since I was the ringmaster in charge of our backstage scene, I worked closely with security to determine who met who and who went where. I deftly maneuvered around record label VIPs, families, wives, agents, dealers, radio DJs, media folk, hangers-on, groupies, and contest winners.

In addition to my recent familiarity with the venue staff, our band and all of us in management were also friendly with the MTV folks. When MTV started, it originally emulated radio. A VJ (video jock) substituted for a DJ (disc jockey) and played videos instead of songs. In creating MTV, the best people in radio (our besties) were hired to make this vision happen. So, between me getting the stagehands out of various jams a few concerts back, Grace and Mickey presenting, and my being grandfathered into MTV coolness, I pretty much had run of the place. But truth be told, outside of Madonna rolling around (tame by today's standards) and running around backstage, I don't remember all that much of the show. It was after the show that things got interesting.

Radio City Music Hall's stage door entrance was located on a small side alley, where limos would relinquish the artists. Just inside, there was a tiny foyer with an elevator to take arrivals upstairs to the rabbit warren of dressing rooms. At the end of the MTV awards show there was an artist stampede to get to their cars. I rode down the rickety little elevator with Grace Slick, to assist in finding her limo. A cocky David Lee Roth and his entourage were in the small space with us. The elevator doors opened to a virtual madhouse. This tiny artist entrance was packed with screaming mangers, yelling publicists, rough-shod road managers, and overwhelmed security trying to control the scene. Everyone was trying to commandeer cars for their artists, most of whom were standing in the frenzy like deer caught in the headlights.

A heavy downpour and the narrowness of the alleyway made the pick-up process agonizingly slow and chaotic. However, one of the beautiful things about working with the generational icon Grace Slick was that Grace commanded the #1 spot no matter where she went. With the help of a burly security guard, I was able to leave David Lee Roth in the dust and deliver her safely and unscathed into her pristine limo, which whisked her away while everyone else waited and fumed.

Eventually all the riffraff cleared out of the backstage area and the stage door entrance calmed down. A security guard came up to me and told me my limo was back. As you can guess, I got very used to rock star amenities. I grabbed my friend RM and we jumped in and went to the official after-party at the Tavern on the Green. From there we went to the St. Regis, where the real party was going on. I sailed into the room of friends, secure in my hipness.

Sitting amongst a group of people I knew from California, was one of my early local rock idols, the Commander. It turned out he and I both had as a friend the man who was hosting this little late-night soiree. The Commander and his band had made some kick ass boogie-rock records in the '70s and were known for legendary over-the-top live club shows. They had cult status in my book, from my earliest days as a new Berkeleyite. Now he and I sat side by side chattering late into the early hours of the morning about how he could resurrect his career.

53

Finally, around 6:30 a.m. RM and I left, and had the limo drive us over to the Hard Rock in mid-town Manhattan. There were a few diehards from the awards show still drinking at the bar. I was wired and not yet tired. I ordered a double Cutty Sark on the rocks and sat back. I cracked open a new pack of cigarettes—my second of the night—and ruminated on the evening.

I felt disturbed by my conversation with the Commander. He had been my musical hero. Now he was just another musician whose career had come and gone. It was an impossible situation for me to appreciate. I felt bad for him, pushing a demo on me. Yet it made sense too. At that moment, I had that mysterious, elusive, intoxicating smell of success, due to my job and status in the industry. Once again, I was reminded of the fickleness of the entertainment business. I looked at the fresh drink in front of me. It was seven-thirty in the morning. I took a healthy sip. Just another day—into night and into day again—in the rock business.

9

Portrait of an Icon

Everyone wants to know what the rock superstars I worked with were like off the stage. I could write reams about my love for the male members of the Jefferson Starship/Starship. Vocally gifted, soulful Mickey Thomas. Phenomenal multi-genre guitarist Craig Chaquico. Incredible multi-instrument-talent Pete Sears. Underrated cultural hero-musician David Freiberg. Impassioned visionary and tribal leader Paul Kantner. Pulsating drummer-singer Donny Baldwin. Renowned English drummer Aynsley Dunbar. I cherish my lifelong friendships with these gentlemen. We traveled the world together and had terrific, fun adventures while achieving a third decade of commercial success for that iconic band.

I'll never forget putting a cassette tape of our unreleased album "Knee Deep in the Hoopla" to the hotel bar after a gig in San Jose, We sang along full-throatily while doing tequila shooters, hoping it would be a success. It sold over a million copies. Or the time guitarist Craig Chaquico and golden-throated vocalist Mickey Thomas and I were in the rental car leaving a gig in Florida. Tempted by the vastness of the parking lot, Craig started doing screaming wheelies, a fun past-time in rental cars, where you drive fast and throw on the emergency brake, which causes the car to do a 180-degree turn. Though we weren't close to any fans and there was no danger of hitting anyone, the erratic nature of our driving caused fans to panic and race away.

When SWAT police officers stopped us, pulling Craig out of the car to handcuff him, the first thing Mickey said was "Don't hurt his hands! Officers, please don't hurt his hands... he's our guitar player!"

Then there was the time David Freiberg got married onstage at an outdoor show in New York City. The marriage didn't last but we got a windfall of publicity out of it. Or when our daring leader Paul Kantner got into a beef with a security guard who was hassling a young female fan, at a concert in Ohio. Paul jumped off the stage and struck the security cop. All hell broke loose after that show with his fellow police officers looking for Paul. Fortunately, our truck driver, the inimitable Fish, spirited him safely away. Pete Sears and his wife Jeannette remained close friends, contributing strong songs to the band's repertoire, while supporting political reform in Guatemala. I became close with all the band's families and friends. They were a good substitute for my own multitudinous family back in Kentucky.

But it is the star of the show, raven-haired beauty Grace Slick, who quietly impacted me. We weren't close friends, but we worked together well through the eighties. I was never a buddy to her, like I was with the guys. I'm sure I annoyed her by treating her as the national treasure she was. But Grace was the most professional celebrity I ever met. She was always on time and prepared for whatever the publicity/promotional machine (me) asked of her. She was also the most closed off. The onus of celebrity always fell on her, despite the talents of the rest of the band. Grace had a constant barrage of people grabbing at her, demanding her time, her attention, or fragments of her celebrity. Incessantly. Relentlessly. Always. Always. Always. I spent as much time surreptitiously being her bodyguard as her publicist.

She managed these intrusions with either an icy, disdain-ful stare or her trademark acerbic humor, depending on the day. But if she committed to a PR event, she always brought her A game. Grace was mostly sober during the years we worked together. Yet I saw the toll the unyielding, constant pressures of fame took on her. I wasn't surprised she had become a heavy drinker. Yet I admired her resilience. Grace has tough exterior cladding that protects a soft, squishy, whimsical heart. I have two memories that illuminate a different side of this rock icon.

In the first we are attending an extravagant Grammy award party hosted by RCA Records. The record label took the entirety of a glittering upscale restaurant for the reception. There were tables overloaded with shrimp, steak, sushi, and other fancy eats, while waiters circulated with an endless supply of cham-pagne. Many other RCA recording artists were in attendance: Diana Ross, Mister Mister, Bruce Hornsby, the Judds. After shaking hands and posing for pictures with a phalanx of record company executives, Grace wanted to leave. We walked to the elevator together so I could see her off safely in the limo. Who stepped into our descending mirrored lift but Diana Ross. She looked like a Black Rapunzel, with a halo of thick, flowing black locks cascading over her shoulders. Diana was wearing a cou-ture gown with a fitted, bejewled silk bodice and an enormous, bouffant skirt of stiff material. Her humongous skirt filled the cramped space. She showed no signs of recognizing Grace, who was in her mid-eighties rock uniform: black jacket, black pants, black boots. Grace's natural beauty not-withstanding, Diana was transcendent in that moment.

While we stood in admiration, Grace, who once modeled couture for a high-end department store, said, "I'd love to be able to wear something like that." There was a tinge of yearning in her voice. Diana looked her up and down with a jaundiced eye, ready to dismiss. But then her look softened. Diana said, "Well you could start with something simple. Maybe a simple long dress." trying to be helpful and kind. I loved Grace's wistfulness at that moment. Her look of longing at something so girly and so far outside her rock persona touched me. Haven't we all fantasized having other looks or maybe even other personas as life carries us onward. Certainly, our choices put us in boxes of our own making. I felt there was so much more behind Grace's words. A deep longing perhaps to get off the Rock & Roll treadmill. Or maybe it was as simple as every woman wanting to be a princess once in a blue moon. Even music icons.

A similar memory comes from a concert at a Texas theme park. A hard afternoon rain made the area between the outdoor stage and the dressing rooms a mud pit. Wooden boards were laid down to make a skinny catwalk through the bog. Grace was leery of traversing such a rickety, snaky path through the muck. She was uncertain how to proceed. Seeing her dilemma, our road manager picked her up in his arms and carried her the fifty yards to the stage. She giggled like a teenager in his arms, her face reflecting unbridled glee and delight. Another *sweet girly* reveal. She was momentarily treated as a female and not just one of the guys running through the wet murk to the stage. For a woman who could quiet a rowdy crowd with a single piercing look, this remains a welcome glimpse of another side of Grace Slick.

Long before pandemics, Grace didn't like shaking hands and she always carried her own pens and sharpies to sign items. She was smart and knew how to survive. Grace often commented she didn't want to be jumping around onstage in her fifties, singing Rock & Roll. She knew she had other talents she wanted to explore. While I didn't understand her sentiments in my thirties, I came to a clear understanding of them in my fifties. What attracts us to music in our youth, ceases to be as meaningful as we mature emotionally. We outgrow the lure of sex, drugs and Rock & Roll. Grace eventually left her successful rock career on her own terms. She let her passion as a painter fuel a second career. Her example resonated with me. In time, I did the same thing—in my own way—loosely based on her playbook. I left a highly visible music career after discovering a passion for hospice work. I've never regretted that move.

10

We Built This City (on Rock & Roll)

San Francisco in the '80s was a kaleidoscope of fun and creative energy. I felt there was so much to do and so little time to do it. Rock, pop, and new wave music was exploding on mainstream radio and MTV. Jefferson Starship/Starship was on top, the nucleus of the band now in their third decade of success, riding high on the success of the hit single "We Built This City on Rock & Roll." We ran a contest on MTV that featured a boat cruise on the Bay, that we loaded with other Bay Area luminaries. Huey Lewis and the News were MTV darlings. Journey was selling out stadiums. Local new wave labels like 415 Records took local acts like Romeo Void and Translator to national prominence. Local bands like Greg Kihn, on Bezerkely Records, had hits on the radio. Nightclubs for music, dancing, comedy, or all the above, were thriving.

Places to live were cheap and plentiful. Everyone could start a band. The local music scene was a cozy club of music biz insiders and hip scenesters, fueled by massive amounts of cocaine, which defined the eighties for many of us. I found myself forced to move into a more isolated mountain cabin in Mill Valley in the late '80s, trying to break my daily drug habit. Yet I continued to be in San Francisco most nights, unwilling to let go of the excitement.

As Jefferson Starship, we played a civic *Save the San Francisco Cable Cars* benefit in the ballroom of the grand Fairmont

Hotel. Comedian Robin Williams opened, as was his wont. Robin was everywhere in SF those days and seemed to be the living embodiment of the San Francisco vibe: smart, clever, and approachable. Most citizens considered SF to be a town of wild possibility and Robin was our Pied Piper.

As Starship, we continued to play high-profile benefits when asked. We played a couple for Jane Fonda and Tom Hayden too. Then Jane put together a "Clean Water Caravan" of Hollywood stars who barnstormed the state for Proposition 65, a proposal to toughen the California toxic waste laws. It was a disparate crew, including Jane and Tom, her brother Peter Fonda, Morgan Fairchild, Shelley Duvall, Ed Begley Jr., and a host of their actor friends. Once again, we were back in the ballroom of the Fairmont Hotel playing to a well-heeled crowd. Afterward, I was told there was an after-concert party upstairs in one of the actor's hotel rooms. I walked in to find my buddies from the band Nightranger chatting with Peter Fonda. Holy Cow! It was Peter's room. I picked up a beer, introduced myself and got into the party mode. Occasionally there would be a knock at the door. I was so used to managing backstage scenes, I automatically went to answer the door and screen whomever was knocking. If they didn't have the name of someone in the room, I wouldn't let them in.

Later, as the crowd thinned out somewhat, Peter and I got to talking. He was as tall as he looks on camera, with an assured presence and gentlemanly manners. His casual affect complimented his good looks. The fact I was acting as the door person to his room made him curious. He told me he knew I was in the "business" by how I took charge. He was comfortable and relaxed. We chatted and did some lines of coke, him speaking of his dad and sister Jane while I listened attentively. Family dominated his conversation. He adored his sister. As I was leaving, we traded numbers. Later I connected him with the Mill Valley Film Festival for a special tribute to *Easy Rider*. He surely deserved all the accolades that came his way.

Amid all this fun and frivolity, I met a tall, cadaverous man from England: MP. While we shagged occasionally, we were both more interested in sussing out interesting scenes than anything else. MP was hanging around an unknown singer songwriter, Chris Isaak, trying to promote him to fame and fortune. MP thought I worked for a "dinosaur" band (a band of older players whose past successes in the '60s and '70s meant nothing in the current '80s. But he knew I was deeply ingrained in the music industry machine. This made me more attractive since he was hoping I could help him on Chris's behalf. MP was brilliant with the hype. He reminded me of Brian Epstein, seemed a reincarnated version of that legendary manager of the Beatles. He was relentless. Every conversation was Chris this and Chris that. One night he even dragged me to a funky music club on California Street so he could convince bass player Rowland Salley (recently relocated from Woodstock, N.Y.) to join Chris's new band. I remember sitting there with Roly (who I had just met) when he turned to me and asked me on the down low if I thought Chris had a legitimate future. I told him yes.

From the vantage point of today, you know Chris Isaak to be an enduringly popular singer with a stream of hits, television shows and movies to his name. His successes are well deserved. But at that time, unsigned and unknown, Chris had to climb his way up the ranks like everyone else chasing success. MP and EJ, Chris's producer, schemed to have Chris and (his newly named band) Silverstone play every Wednesday night a dive bar in the Haight Ashbury called the Nightbreak. The Haight had a revitalized new wave, punkish cachet and was working an upswing. The Nightbreak had a cramped, low-rise stage and held 50-75 patrons. MP was sure if they could fill the Nightbreak with fans, it would be just like the Beatles at the Cavern Club, with screaming girls and wild success. I was busy with my band Starship touring across the country, collaborating with promoters and MTV, and dealing with fund raisers. Although I liked the demo tapes Chris was recording, I didn't pay much attention to yet another of MP's endless promotional ideas.

One night I was in my apartment on the Buena Vista Park side of Castro, having dinner with a large group of friends. Around 9 p.m. I got a frantic call from MP. They were down the hill at the Nightbreak. It was the very first night of their weekly shows and *no one was there*. Could I come down and bring my friends? Sure. We trundled down to the place only to see the band standing around waiting to see if anyone would show up. Once we got there they settled down and played, and we heartedly applauded—all eight of us, plus a few of the band's pals.

I was taken with the live outfit. Not only did they all play well but they fit Chris perfectly. Chris had a wonderful voice, a clever stage personality, and wrote sophisticated, memorable songs. Texan Kenny Dale Johnson was an impeccable drummer and harmony singer. Rowland Salley was an exquisite bass player. Jimmy Wilsey, the guitar player, nailed their style. They were a mash up of raves, rock, and crooning, unique in their sound. I was sold.

From that night forward I rarely missed a Wednesday night for the next six months. MP flogged that show and pestered people until folks started coming of their own volition. Chris and the band were that good, and yes, Chris was that cute. The hipster girls came as designed, which meant the guys followed. It started to get packed on a regular basis with lines out the door. The band started holding a small two-top table in the rear, with a sign that read "Reserved for Nadine." Being a music insider, it was fun watching the industry discover Chris. First came some small Warner Bros. Records reps. Then the big-time booking agents from Monterey Peninsula Artists. Then big-time Warner Records guys. Eventually everything happened exactly as MP and EJ had hoped. Soon the rest of the world discovered Chris Isaak and Silvertone.

Music continued to be a defining piece of San Francisco culture until the 2000s when tech companies began to over-run/sweep into the City like a tsunami. The tech migration changed the personality of the city. Music clubs sat on valuable real estate that could be turned into needed condominiums and apartments. Cheap rehearsal places were turned into more living spaces. Musicians were forced out of the city to urban suburbs in their quest to continue their artistic endeavors. Tech concerns like Twitter, Uber, Lyft, Airbnb, Yelp, and other behemoths (Apple and Google are just a short drive away in Silicon Valley) eventually moved in and took over San Francisco. And that's okay. Every generation gets a turn in our beloved City by the Bay. I believe that's what makes San Francisco unique, its ability to shape shift with each succeeding generational cohort that arrives. It started with the Gold Rush and has never really ended. It's thrilling to be part of this continuum—this history of travelers, seekers, artists, and futurists.

11

Midnight Meeting at Rock Mansion

My experience finding and returning a *lost Super Bowl* ring has become a popular story that never ceases to astonish friends. It was that sublime time in the mid-80s when I was a Rock & Roll insider. Working for the rock band Jefferson Starship (later simply Starship,) we were in the middle of a run of Top Ten hit songs (Sara, We Built This City, Nothing's Gonna Stop Us Now) commanding the airwaves, and enjoying the rewards of success and celebrity. As Director of Promotion and Publicity for the group, I was a highly visible ringleader in the middle of the Rock & Roll circus. My life was the band. Everything I did revolved around their activities.

It was winter, mid-80s, when the band had a series of weekend shows at a Lake Tahoe casino. Today it's normal for bands to play casinos, especially vintage acts. But in1985 few rock bands played casinos, which were still the domain of "Vegas" type entertainers like Wayne Newton or Tony Bennett. Back in the 80s though, it was a hugely coveted entertainment gig. Not only were you paid extremely well but the amenities were first class. No reconfigured arena locker room with folding chairs and deli-tray. The casino had a plush living room style backstage with private dressing rooms, swanky couches and mirrors, champagne on hand. All band members and management (including me) were given luxe suites with expansive lake views. Food and drink vouchers worth hundreds of dollars were given to each of us daily. I would order a dozen drinks at a time from room service, entertaining the parade of folks through my suite, wrapped in my plush hotel robe, and lounging on the humongous bed. Everyone liked playing Lake Tahoe. Easy money—take the elevator down from your VIP suite, shake a few hands and walk onstage. Easy times.

One of my best friends at the time was Mark Davis, whose Dad Al owned the Raiders. As a friend, Mark would normally be with us at Tahoe. But business concerns and scouting the Senior Bowl had him in Japan. Circumstances had changed with the Raiders in the eighties. They had left Oakland and moved to Los Angeles. Mark had followed suit and moved to a house in Hermosa Beach. I'd often go down for Raider games and occasionally stayed at his house. During the move, one of Mark's Super Bowl rings was stolen. The Raiders had won Super Bowls in 1977, 1981, and 1984. Mark had rings to commemorate each win. The missing ring was especially sentimental: 1977 marked their first Super Bowl win. Mark reported the theft and had NFL security looking for the ring. Time went by but the ring did not show up.

Fast forward to Lake Tahoe and the Starship gig, mid-80s. I was backstage managing the typically chaotic post-show dressing room juggle. The scene was winding down and the mass of band friends was dispersing. A non-descript blond-haired guy of normal height and regular build had come in with a group of Mickey Thomas' Tahoe friends, always a fast crowd. As Mr. Non-Descript sauntered by me on his way out, I happened to glance at his hand and notice him wearing a Raiders Super Bowl ring. Would it have been noticeable to a casual fan? Probably not, but I was Raider family and knew these things. What happened next was pure destiny. It still gives me chills, all these many years later.

Whenever I recall this indelible moment, time stands still, the memory rendered in slow motion. Mr. Non-Descript walks by me to leave the dressing room. I zero in on the Raider ring I had only glanced at earlier. Mr. Non-Descript is reaching for the door handle. His back is to me. I ask from about ten feet away, "You're wearing a Raider Super Bowl ring?" "Yep," he answers, looking at me over his shoulder, hand still on the door handle. Right then, the Spirit, that beneficent entity, moves me to spontaneously blurt "That's Mark Davis' Super Bowl ring." Continuing the jaw-dropping scene we had going, Mr. Non-Descript says "Why yes, it is," in an arrogant tone, completely non-plussed.

I covered the distance between us in two steps. Obviously, this guy wasn't concealing the fact it was Mark Davis' ring. "Wow, how did you get it," I asked him, pretending to be impressed. Then Mr. Non-Descript compounded the infraction by picking an implausible story to tell me about how the ring came to him. Unaware that I knew Mark, he was boastful. "Oh, Mark Davis gave it to someone, who gave it to someone. That someone owed me money and gave me the ring instead." He held up his hand and showed it off proudly.

I couldn't pussyfoot around any longer. I told him how the ring had been stolen from Mark's home and how Mark had NFL security looking for the ring. I told him Mark was in Japan but wanted his ring back. Mr. Non-Descript didn't bat an eye, only shifted gears, and adopted a new tack. "That's wonderful," he gushed, "I'd love to sell the ring back to him." Sell a stolen Super Bowl ring back to its rightful owner is a rich concept, but I went with it. I told him we'd be in touch after Mark got home.

To be honest, my mind was spinning. How had I known that was Mark Davis' Super Bowl ring, with only such a brief glimpse? I was floored. At that time, I feared anything that smacked of Spirit, intuition, or other-worldly sensibility. Yet those words had leapt out of my mouth unbidden. Still, I was uncomprehending of the lesson here. All I knew was I was super-excited and tingly. I had found Mark's ring! I knew how thrilled he would be.

Since this was the mid-80s and cell phones had yet to be invented, I couldn't call Mark in Japan. But I left a message on his home phone for when he returned. I gave him the lowdown on Tahoe, what mutual friends had been there and how great guitarist Craig Chaquico had played. At the end, I casually added "Oh by the way, I found your ring. Some guy was wearing it who lives in Sausalito. Call me when you get home." You know just another gig run-down and by the way, some guy is wearing your ring. Nothing special. Talk about burying the lede!

Mark got back from Japan and checked his messages. He heard my message and called me immediately. It was 4:00 in the afternoon. I was lying on my bed when the phone rang. I was eager to hear from him and wanted to hear about Japan. "What do you mean you found my ring?" were the first words out of his mouth. I gave him the lowdown and he said he wanted to see the guy right away. He wanted his ring back. Calls were made and a meeting was set up for eleven that evening at the Airplane house—where we had our Starship offices.

This was the perfect setting. Back in the day, the name of the band that preceded both Jefferson Starship, and Starship, was Jefferson Airplane. They were the first successful psyche-delic rock band out of San Francisco. Flush with money in the late 60s, they bought a three-story Colonial Revival style home across from Golden Gate Park. It served as home and office to the bands for many years. By the mid-80s, the *Mansion* was an iconic San Francisco landmark that still served as office for the band and management. Since my office was there, I took people over there at all hours of the day and night. We would party and shoot pool, while I showed off the pink-silk tapestry wall coverings, the 1906 stained glass window, the psychedelic paint in the kitchen, and the octagonal bedroom on the third floor.

I drove to the meeting with trepidation. My roommate MC was with me. The black and white tiled front porch with its giant gold Doric columns and painted ceiling was bathed in dark shadow. Wispy, cold fog drifted by in the silence of the winter night. I opened the huge front door and immediately turned on the hall lights. Unlike other nights when I had no qualms about being there, this night had a sinister quality to it. There was a tension in the air that surrounding this meeting. I slinked through the huge silent rooms feeling like Nancy Drew—without the Hardy Boys—except these were much higher stakes.

After a short while, I opened the massive wooden front door, letting Mark and a friend inside. Ten minutes later Mr. Non-Descript walked in with a friend. I made nervous introductions as I led everyone into the pool room. This richly decorated room had rare birds-eye maple wainscoting. The flocked green velvet wallpaper was original from 1904. An antique lamp fixture hung low over a 1908 pool table covered with red felt. The windows were shielded with heavy, tasseled drapes that I had closed earlier for privacy. The exchange began.

Twenty minutes later Mark had his ring back and all was well with the world. This long-ago event will be forever etched in my soul's timeline. In an earlier decade I had an almost deadly experience because I *had not listened* to my intuition. I had suffered from that. Now again, another possibly scary situation; and yet, it had turned out positively. Could I really trust this inner voice? Was it there to benefit me?

What a stunning message amid my crazy life. It took me a few more years to grasp the enormity of this lesson. It was not until I committed to personal counseling that I came to haltingly understand the benevolent, guiding role of Spirit in my life. Maybe I *could* trust myself. Perhaps I *could* trust my inner compass.

Later Mark gifted me with the matching woman's pendant in gratitude and appreciation for finding his ring. I was both humbled and wowed by his kindness. Did I deserve such a valuable present? The actual face of the Super Bowl ring serves as the medallion. Black onyx, a diamond football, more accent diamonds, and silver. Twenty-seven diamonds to be exact. It's a big, heavy conspicuous piece of jewelry. I always get a reaction when I wear this unique pendant. It's simply gorgeous.

Over the years the pendant has become my most treasured talisman. Not because of its appraised value or even the *coolness* factor—which cannot be overestimated. Not even because it speaks to the depths of a very dear, ongoing friendship— Thank you, Mark. No. It is my most treasured talisman because it represents a significant juncture in my life. That spontaneous moment of decisive intuition became a powerful thunderbolt of discovery for me. It helped set me back on the road to trusting myself. Once I cracked open that door of trusting Spirit, my life began to change permanently for the better. That is the real gift here.

12

The Daily Grind

A gentle chirping invades my consciousness. I reach for the bedside phone from a dead sleep. It's my 8:45 a.m. wake-up call. I am in an anonymous hotel with the hit band Jefferson Starship, and we are on a concert tour. I am groggy with lack of sleep. It takes me about fifteen minutes to rouse myself. My message light is flashing with a handful of calls since 8:00 a.m. this morning, but hotel staff faithfully followed my "do not disturb" instructions.

I throw off the covers and rinse my face. My morning routine is basic. Teeth, face, washcloth dabs at privates and pits, brush hair. Shower comes in the next city. I hurriedly gather my clothes and throw them back into my suitcases. Bags will be picked up at 9:30 a.m. and must be ready by that time. Our road manager calls me at 9:00 a.m. to reconfirm I should be in the lobby at 9:45 a.m. There are no cell phones, so after dressing and securing my bags, I start returning the messages left for me from the record company, promoters, newspaper writers and radio folks. I may have started as a publicist but over time I took on additional responsibilities as well: management rep, radio promotion liaison, record company liaison, tour press, national press. Basically, if you wanted to do anything with the band, you had to go through me first.

By the time I reach the lobby all the band is there except Bill Thompson, the manager. He's usually on the phone and

71

running late. We ride to the airport recounting the night before. Upon reaching our terminal we scatter like roaches. Some of the guys head to the bar for Bloody Mary's and "sky dogs" ---airport hot dogs. They are de rigueur after a night of carousing. Others head to the gate, our road manager sticking close to Grace, so she doesn't get bothered by fans.

I head to a bank of public phones. Using a long-distance calling card, I take over a phone booth, itinerary out, notebook at the ready. I start dialing and do not stop until I hear boarding announced for our flight. I juggle calls not only about tonight's concert, but also tomorrow's show, the one the day after that, the shows in the weeks to come, and so forth. I actively work a four to twenty-week window of concerts at any one time. I love touring work the absolute best.

Plane rides were mostly quiet, people listening to their Walkmans (small, portable cassette players,) reading or sleeping. There was never enough sleep on the road. All would be well until landing. Then drummer Donny Baldwin could be counted on to start yelling "We're coming in too fast! We're coming in too fast!" right before the wheels touched down. This would put our fellow passengers anxiously on alert, while the band snickered. He would exhale a loud, audible sigh of relief after landing safely, for the crowd's benefit.

Arriving at our next hotel, I am greeted with a yet another fistful of messages upon check-in. After entering my hotel room, I make more phone calls while awaiting delivery of my bags. There was that time in Houston when the bellman knocked on my door with my bags. That summer I was using a set of soft-sided duffels. I opened the door to see the bell person holding one of the bags at arm's length. "Maaaaam," he exclaimed "There something alive in this here bag!" I quickly took it from him and shut the door. It was my trusty vibrator that somehow had gotten switched on while in transit. It was vibrating. Non-plussed, I made one of the roadies go out and buy me fresh batteries.

About 5 p.m. I wander up to BT's room to talk things over. We do a line of coke and compare notes. I let him know who would be there from the record company, what radio personnel would be attending, and what press we were expecting. We go over upcoming shows and discuss ticket sales. If a show wasn't selling well, I might coordinate more radio promotions or publicity around the concert. We catch up on all business matters. Then he thrusts a torn piece of paper into my hands with some guest names scribbled on it.

Returning to my room, I order a light meal and drinks. I rarely drink during the day but order wine and beer to have something in my room for after the show, when room service is closed. While waiting for room service to be delivered, I shower and decide on the night's outfit. I call our road manager BL about passes and the "meet and greets" where music industry personnel, radio DJs, record store folks, record company reps, and newspaper writers would meet the band, along with contest winners and fans. BL tells me to be in the lobby at 7:00 p.m. o'clock. We arrive at the venue about ninety minutes before the band goes onstage as the headliner.

Because I am so close to the record label representatives around the country, one of them is usually there waiting for me. If newspaper writers are coming, I find them and kibbutz. Newspapers ruled in those days. Radio stations were equally powerful. Often, competing stations were at the same show and I had to use all my powers of diplomacy to insure they all got equal treatment.

I go to the production office and say hello to the promoter's crew, check for any guest list snafus, check for friends or family of the band, and wander into the dressing room. I would let everyone know what and who to expect that night, post show. (Now, most bands wisely do "meet and greets' before the show. I wish we had thought of that back in the '80s!)

I leave the band about ten minutes before they hit the stage, to give them quiet time. Mickey Thomas is running scales in the bathroom. Grace Slick is smoking her final cigarette. Paul Kantner is smoking a doobie. Donny Baldwin is drumming on drum pads to warm up. Craig Chaquico is sliding into his leather pants. Aynsley Dunbar, when he was the drummer, might be already on stage checking his kit. David Freiberg and Pete Sears had their own pre-show routines. I would take any special guests we had and get them situated on the side of the stage, instructing various crew to watch out for them. Then I would position myself at the foot of the stairs leading to the stage. As the lights dimmed, I would wish them good luck as they climbed up to the stage, straight out of the movie Almost Famous.

I watch the first song from the side of the stage. I then go out into the audience and walk around, taking in the crowd and doing a quick head count while checking the sound from different areas of the venue. I might mosey over to the soundboard in the middle of the audience, where the sound man and lighting director are manning their controls. Their crews started setting up sound and lighting equipment early that morning. I then drift back to the side of the stage and sit on a road case for a few more songs. Later I go into the dressing room to get myself a beer. I find our manager talking with the promoter. I sit with them and discuss business or share industry gossip. There is nothing I like more than talking music business. I snort another line or two with them. Then I would hear a fave song and go back to the stage with beers for everyone standing on the sidelines.

When the bass or drum solos came in the set, I always try to be on the side of the stage. Band members gulp water, beer, shots of hard liquor. Someone takes a puff of a cigarette or joint, maybe a bump of cocaine. Towels are at the ready for them to wipe the sweat off their bodies. Those stage lights are hot! After the solos, it's a greatest hits dash to the finish.

As soon as the show is finished and the encore over, the band returns to their dressing room dripping wet. I'm going to wait until they've had a chance to change into dry clothes before bringing them into the hospitality room. I go to manage the post-show chaos. There is bedlam at the side of the stage. The record label rep corrals their people from radio and record stores. The news writers huddle together in a pack. I first grab family/friends who sat out front and bring them backstage into the hospitality room. I let the band members know their friends and family are backstage. Eventually everyone is in the hospitality room, meeting and greeting and getting pictures taken for trade magazines or posterity. It's a zany, crazy, wonderful scene, worthy of my ringmaster talents. I'm famous among record label reps for remembering an unending number of names for introductions to the band.

Not all the band does the meet and greets. Grace usually gets special dispensation, except for bigwigs and major cities. She's met enough people in her lifetime. Paul Kantner is usually amenable, friendly, and always has an eclectic list of visitors. Mickey Thomas uses his southern charm to graciously welcome everyone. He is always amiable, professional and a dream. Occasionally I take him to throat doctors in various cities to keep his gifted vocal instrument in working condition. I admire his fortitude as scopes are thrust down his throat (yikes). Craig is always upbeat, willing to pose for pictures and a natural charmer. David, Pete, Donny, Aynsley are good sports too, despite the repetition and routine from city to city.

Usually, the band leaves the venue at staggered times. Some band members like to hang out backstage to come down from the adrenaline rush. Other like to retire to their hotel rooms to decompress safely. Paul Kantner always "dresses" his hotel room with scarves over lamps and has windows that open. It's homey and atmospheric, no matter what hotel is hosting us.

I'm in the last group to leave, after having invited a gang of folks back to the hotel bar for a post-show cocktail. These are the absolute best times. The band will take over multiple tables in the bar. If the roadies are staying overnight, they will join us. There are a few shy but determined groupies in the lobby who steadily work their way into the group. There are different pairings amongst these tables. The record label reps jostle to get close to band members. I'm entertaining radio DJs or writers. Maybe I'm picking someone up that night, maybe not. When the bar closes, we go to someone's room and continue talking. The party lasts as long as there are alcohol and drugs and then everyone crashes.

There was the time after playing Merriweather Post Pavilion outside Washington, D.C. I was entertaining three men: a music writer from Baltimore, a record label rep from D C, and a promoter rep from the venue. All were flirting with me wildly. After some male sparring, the promoter rep picked up my red high heeled shoe, poured champagne in it and drank from it, an extraordinary burst of testosterone bravado. I felt like Scarlet O'Hara with the Tarleton Twins vying for my attentions. Heady times.

If we are in the middle of a three-day weekend run, I usually go balls to the walls then collapse on Monday, after traveling to the next concert town. I buy trashy magazines and candy bars in the lobby shop, order room service and turn off my phone until the next day. Waking up on Tuesday, not having to travel is a treat. I have a leisurely breakfast before getting on the phone. I have my cigarettes, ashtray, notebook, itineraries, dirty dishes, empty glasses, and assorted papers spread around my king bed. I won't leave that room until I go to the show that night. Tuesday nights are never spent in a major market or large city, so the pressure is lessened for that evening's concert.

I once had a writer/date come to my room in NYC. We were supposed to be going out in Manhattan. I opened the door still in my bathrobe, cigarette ashtrays overflowing, the detritus of a day on the phone visible. Dirty plates on the floor, clothes scattered. I remember him asking me if I spent most days in rooms like that and I said yes. He shook his head over my unhealthy lifestyle. I was oblivious to his concerns and probably did another line of coke in the bathroom while he waited.

And so, it goes. Unless I am taking Craig Chaquico to a radio station in front of the concert. Usually those were done either early morning or late afternoon so he could appear during "drive time," the commute hours when most folks listen to terrestrial radio. Those were fun but murderously early in the morning. Craig Chaquico was/is masterful on the radio, conveying excitement and good vibes while telling stories in perfect sound bites. Once I got to know the RCA record reps and trusted them, I could stay in the room on the phone, while they ferried Craig about town. If it is Mickey, Grace, or Paul, I always go with them to oversee the activity at hand.

I'm happy I got to experience my road trips in the eighties. Although folks thought the music business had become too commercial by then, in reflection, it now seems quaint. It's changed so much in forty years. The current business of live performing is a massive yet smooth running machine with tour busses, backstage catering, lavishly decorated dressing rooms and private jets flying you home each evening. Concerts, which used to be under the aegis of a phalanx of regional promoters, are now controlled by a few large multi-national concerns. There is much less record label involvement, fewer radio stations and no stores (since streaming put them out of business.) Artists have struck gold offering expensive ticket packages of high-end meet and greets, complete with private bars and articles of clothing. These are no longer free. Unlike back in *the day*, you *pay* to meet the artist now.

PART THREE

Flashbacks to Move Forward

Sometimes it's necessary to review your past before you can move forward. That is what the 1990s represented for me: a chance to reclaim my past while moving into the future. At that time, I also suffered the loss of my Mother and my best friend JK. And I met the man who would become my partner in life. I searched for how to make my mark in Rock & Roll and the city of San Francisco. Nadine's Wild Weekend music showcase festival was the result. I tended old wounds that had never healed by confronting a scarred past that had threatened to keep me in its confining thrall. I sought to resolve long-standing issues of fear and insecurity. I quit hiding my doubts behind my ballsy personality and bravado. The result was that I moved forward through disparate stages of living that decade. Those years were both tumultuous and rewarding. I think you will relate, seeing behind my curtain of change and growth...

13

Nineties Music

If I was committed to the Jefferson Starship in the eighties, the nineties represented new beginnings for me. I loved touring across the United States and around the world to England, Europe, and Japan. The Starship band and crew were family, friends, lovers, and confidants all rolled into one. But when Grace Slick left the band, I knew the writing was on the wall. I realized I was in a dead-end job. Despite the expanded management responsibilities, I took on through the years, I was always vastly underpaid working for the band, contenting myself with the glam and the glitter. After tasting the highlife for a decade with a legacy band, I turned my attention to the future.

On the professional Rock & Roll side of things, I opened an office in a hip music business complex in the San Francisco. I was respected in the industry and had no difficulty finding record label friends to hire me to help promote their bands on the road. I worked with a variety of labels promoting their touring artists with radio stations and record stores. I worked most notably and closely with the talented Melissa Etheridge, The Eels, the godfather of English blues, John Mayall, Steve Miller, and a host of other acts I've forgotten. I was best friends with tour managers across the country.

Additionally, the Bay Area was teeming with a new crop of young, talented musicians. It was a rich local scene I stepped into as a music pro. I found my experience beneficial to regional musical artists just starting out. I had a good eye for a new musician's potential. My advice was down to earth and valuable. I became a denizen of the night, haunting nightclubs and checking out the various *scenes* around town. Live music was always my bailiwick. I enjoyed seeing baby bands hone their chops in nightclubs large and small while I hung at the bar.

This new decade brought me a broad range of successes and failures. I co-produced the first official Rock & Roll Fantasy Camp held in San Francisco and featuring Mick Fleetwood and Craig Chaquico. We got it on *ABC Sunday Night News* and a feature in *HELLO* magazine in Britain. Later, the founder relinquished the name "Rock & Roll Fantasy Camp," and it was scooped up by Ringo Starr's manager, who parlayed it into widespread success.

I developed a huge interest in alternative, indie music after leaving the Jefferson Starship. I became a consultant to Broadcast Music Inc. (BMI, a music licensing company), beginning a fruitful fifteen-year collaboration. Shortly thereafter I started producing "BMI New Music" showcases regularly in San Francisco, Seattle, Portland, and Los Angeles. A showcase was an evening of multiple singers or bands performing short musical sets of their best songs. The musicians who were chosen were up and coming regional talent. The event was geared to the music industry. Record label reps, along managers, producers, and attorneys, would attend hoping to find a new act to sign to their label or business. I got to know the music milieus in each of those cities intimately, not only rock, grunge, and indie music, but also R&B, soul, and rap. BMI had a terrific staff (who deserve tons of credit) and did phenomenal outreach to the industry. We presented hundreds of bands over the years, helping them create connections in their quest for music business partnerships. Bands like Counting Crows, Third Eye

Blind, and Train found huge mainstream success. I even showcased young Beyonce Knowles and Kelly Rowland when they were in the teen group, Girls Tyme, which later morphed into Destiny's Child.

The showcases took on a life of their own. Seattle was a heavy scene for heroin. Once, while trying to find my local contact, I walked into a dim, smokey heroin shooting gallery above the nightclub by mistake. Portland was always a super music town and one of the first bands I showcased there later grew into the popular indie group, the Dandy Warhols. In San Francisco, competition was always fierce. One of my favorite acts remains Storm Large—who would partially strip onstage for the college boys while bringing down the house vocally. Storm later successfully stood out in a televised music competition. Today she occasionally sings with Pink Martini, performing classical, jazz, and pop music around the world.

Beyond the showcases, I put Jefferson Starship guitarist Craig Chaquico and the premier New Age label Higher Octave together for a successful collaboration. Craig spent much of the nineties as a superstar in the New Age radio field, his talents morphing successfully into that genre.

I managed a couple of talented local acts too. Elton John signed young singer Ryan Downe to his resuscitated Rocket Records. Ryan was dramatic, earnest, and darling. I was able to get Ryan an opening slot on a long tour with those English diehards, the Who. It didn't help him sell any records. Elton's experiment in reviving his label fell apart and Ryan's career with it. But not before we both had tea with Elton and his husband David in their New York City suite. We also went backstage to visit Elton at a concert in Oakland. Gracing the wall of his highly decorated backstage lounge was a giant portrait of Diana, Princess of Wales (This was shortly after she had died.).

I also was able to get Her Majesty the Baby, a band with two front women and a two-man rhythm section, a record deal with a small indie label. They were popular with the indie and LGBT crowd. They were signed by respected record man Paul Atkinson, an original member of the English rock group, the Zombies, who I had worked with at RCA Records. Paul's new label folded right as they were releasing the Her Majesty CD as a CD-ROM, yet another music-tech breakthrough that crashed and burned.

I wasn't too disappointed. I found managing baby bands challenging work with little immediate payback, emotional or financial. I continued my search to solidify my unique niche in the scene. Despite my outsize presence, my company remained tiny. Just a few dedicated, talented part-timers and me. I was a small but respected player in a big field. There were hundreds of companies like mine that were able to successfully live off the giant music business teat. I was in Los Angeles regularly in the nineties attending diverse music industry events and hanging on the Sunset Strip. One of my most treasured memories follows.

14

Muhammad Ali at Elton's Party

I attended Elton J's Oscar party multiple times in the mid-90s. Elton's Academy Award extravaganza was always crowded with musicians, actors, and celebrities. Bruce Springsteen was there. Oscar winner Angela Bassett. It was that kind of night. Elton is the penultimate host and fund raiser and this party in Los Angeles was no different.

Suddenly Muhammad Ali walks in with an entourage who doubled as his security. Although he was still upright and walking, he had perceptible head tremors from Parkinson's. This did nothing, however, to lessen his immediate, immense magnetism. Without people even turning around, the air was suddenly crisper. His mere entry electrified the space. This scrum of protectors moved Ali smoothly down the entry hall as the jaded attendees parted like the Red Sea.

I was about six people away, outside his inner group as he passed, soon to be forever lost in the heavily fortified VIP room. Although I was sassily dressed up in a rock-star-awards-show-benefit outfit, simply being in proximity to this man reduced me to a shrieking, yelling thirty-something person shouting "Ali I'm from Louisville! I'm from *Luavulle*! I'm from *Luavulle*," using the city's local vernacular to prove my authenticity. I muscled through the throng toward him.

Miraculously, the scrum stopped. I stood a good six feet tall in my heels and leaned precariously over two or three members of Ali's camp who were between us. As I did so, Ali regally offered me his cheek. It was as ritualistic as the prince stopping to receive his just homage, nothing false about it. He deigned to stop for me!

I was just hardly-barely able to reach my lips to his smooth beautiful face. His skin was dry and soft. Soft and cool. We had a gentle brushing of skins. A wisp of connection. Fleeting. I still can remember exactly how his skin felt on my lips.

I raised my head back in wonderment, slightly stunned. His head righted, bobbing, and the pack started their inexorable march forward. *The Greatest* was in the house.

15

Nineties Personal Life

My life was different now. Through restorative therapy and diligent work on my part, I had changed some self-destructive habits and was trusting myself more. I had wrestled a nasty cocaine habit (an occupational hazard in the eighties) to the ground by relocating to a mountaintop cabin in a suburb outside San Francisco. I was no longer picking up hunky guys at stoplights and casually taking them home at my whim. In a surprise turn of events, and with the Spirit's help, I had met my life partner, Honey.

Meeting the love of my life was not without difficulties. Honey and I originally met at a Kentucky Derby party in San Francisco in 1984. We were coincidentally from the same hometown of Louisville and tangentially from the same social milieu there. It was instant dislike on my part. He was young, loud, and cocky. I dismissed him. A couple of years later we met again under more favorable circumstances. I had just bought a Bing-cherry red two-door sportscar. I had it parked in the middle of Divisadero Street, door wide open, stereo blaring, flashing my "hide- away" headlights on and off with glee. My future Honey came over with BD, a mutual friend, to see my roommate MC for party favors. I made them sit in the passenger seat while I extolled the virtues of my first brand-new automobile. We all retired to the apartment and had a few beers. This time he made a better impression. Unfortunately, he liked the wrong sports team. There is fierce rivalry between fans of the University of Kentucky and the University of Louisville. I had nothing but disdain for University of Kentucky fans. Oops. When our third meeting came about a couple of years later, the Spirit demanded I pay attention to this man despite my myopic shallowness.

I was supporting a small but prestigious benefit concert at a club in the revitalized Haight Ashbury. I had provided guest tickets to our mutual friend, BD, who then invited Honey to join him at the show. I bustled around the show in work mode, wearing my game face, greeting, and organizing. Suddenly Honey approached me in true southern gentleman fashion and thanked me for the tickets. I chatted with him perfunctorily and walked away to greet the next person. I was stopped abruptly by an *insistent tap* on my shoulder, wordlessly urging me to go back and talk to that man. *Stop. Go back. Stop. Go back. Talk to him.*

This time I listened to the Spirit and simply followed directions. Surprising both of us, I went and re-engaged Honey in conversation. This was a man I would normally have over-looked. He was not a music biz insider. While extremely cute, he was also very straight looking. Not my usual type. I found him unexpectedly conversant and funny. Shortly thereafter, I invited him to sit at my VIP table. I was powerfully attracted to him that night, crossing and uncrossing my mini-skirted legs over and over in enticement. Unfortunately, I had business clients in town, and he was renovating his new condominium. Our timing was off once again.

Life moved on and I forgot about him. At the time, I was overseeing a weekly nightclub residency in North Beach for a baby band, Noonday Underground. Having forgotten I had mentioned these ongoing shows to Honey, I was floored when he unexpectedly showed up a few weeks later. Floored or not, this was the beginning of us. We were like two magnets colliding. I had finally listened to the Spirit, with marvelous results.

Once we got together, Honey and I were a good match. We both liked to drink, party, and listen to music. Even more significant, here was a man who respected me—more than I respected myself. Before driving up to my mountain cabin for our first assignation, he made sure I was comfortable with his intentions. I responded in my typically profane way, dismissing his ridiculous concerns.

Honey and I moved in together after a couple of years, a momentous occasion for two adults so determinedly single. We certainly didn't expect to fall in love. Each of us were virulently anti-marriage. Which is why I was shocked speechless by his marriage proposal. Truth be told, the night before he surprised me with a ring, we had a massive argument over whether to trim or not trim plants in the garden. I stormed out of the house and drove off angry as a hornet. And yet, here we are—all these happily married years later—our bickering and egos mostly tamped down by the two keys to happiness: *love and laughter.* As Honey likes to say, "Love is laughter. Laughter is love." So even though we annoy the heck out of each other sometimes, we still laugh, love, and enjoy each other immensely. Partners for life.

Being in a relationship with a man who was my equal encouraged me—while also challenging me. His is a creative soul—carving stone sculptures, painting watercolors, writing haiku or sonnets, all the while working full-time in the stone and building trades. His art challenged me to develop my own struggling sense of creativity. Although I had long felt intellectually equal to any working artist, defining my own medium of artistic expression remained elusive.

Honey's support also sustained me through a series of personal losses that flummoxed me. I dipped a toe back into the Catholic Church after these losses, sparking a renewed interest in spiritual reading and spiritual activities. I also determined to understand my fears better. Despite therapy in the latter eighties, I often would be overwhelmed by insecurity, unable to make the simplest business call. I would find myself too timid to speak with a necessary contact. Despite my outgoing personality, I sometimes felt unimportant, inferior. I read self-help books and went to seminars designed to make me a stronger, more confident person. It wasn't until I discovered *The Artist's Way*, by Julia Cameron, that I began the next step of my irrevocable climb away from fear and into a more authentic version of me.

The book is a "quasi-spiritual manual for creative recovery," as its author Julia Cameron puts it. Her series of creative exercises has been a lodestar to blocked writers and other artistic hopefuls for more than a quarter of a century. Cameron's main tool is a writing exercise called Morning Pages. Morning Pages requires you write three pages, by hand, first thing in the morning, about whatever comes to mind. A variety of authors and entrepreneurs now swear by this method. Elizabeth Gilbert, Patricia Cornwell, Pete Townshend, and Alicia Keys have all noted the influence of Morning Pages on their work.

When I started The *Artist's Way* in the mid-nineties, I kept bumping up against the ceiling of my own protective shell. My personal creativity wanted out, but it had become trapped in the hardy carapace I had built for my inner wounds. The exercises in the book helped explain many of my self-sabotaging habits. It expanded my horizons and gave my imagination breathing room. A few years of writing every morning cracked the walls of my defenses and helped tamp down my inner critic. Slowly, a potential future came into view—which is how I wrote my way to becoming the *Godmother of Rock* at *Nadine's Wild Weekend* music festival. Before the festival could start, however, I had to overcome some lingering personal demons.

16

Vanquishing the Predator at Last

The predator came for me in the early evening of a cold, bright, autumnal night. He stole my breezy confidence and self-assuredness. Afterward, I was left scrambling for the safety of anonymity, fearful of darkness—and always on red alert. I would never again be the first to answer. I would often doubt myself. There was no rest for my fight or flight synapses for much of my adult life.

What I remember is the cold concrete under my bare bottom. That and the white pearl-handled pistol staring me in the face while he grunted on top of me. The barrel was a gaping black hole. He held that gun against my head, the entire time of the rape. If I turned my head slightly from staring down that malevolent tunnel, I could see the twinkling stars above, which seemed odd, as the urban light normally washed out the starry night skies.

I was both in my body and out of it, looking down on the scene. I can see him on top of me, the pork pie hat incongruous on his head. His stocky body pushing away, while holding my arms fast to my sides. The paleness of my limbs against the frosty cement ground. He kept telling me not to make a sound or he would kill me. I pretended to enjoy what he was doing to me. I was numb with terror and unfeeling physically, except for the chill on my nude limbs.

I realized with a sinking heart he was going to kill me, no matter what I did. There was no doubt in my mind. My life flashed before my eyes in a millisecond, just like they say. Every memory compressed into an instance of complete understanding. Then an incredible feeling of peace came over me. Calmness replaced fear and swaddled me like a warm blanket. Suddenly I was not afraid of dying. I gave myself up to it wholeheartedly.

And boom! That's when he jumped up and broke the spell. Abruptly getting off me, he told me to "Stay still!" and ran. I heard him climb the chain link fence bordering the alley. I was sure he was coming back with his friends to kill me. I lay there silently awaiting my fate, too paralyzed with fear to move.

Minutes went by, maybe seconds, before I cautiously raised my head and sat up, looking around. I was unclothed and alone, about twenty yards off the sidewalk leading to my dorm. I was hidden by bushes, back in a corner. A scant three houses away from my co-ed dorm, yet emotionally miles away. Violated and abandoned, all my wounds felt hidden in a tightly wrapped bundle of nerves. I've never fully unwrapped that bundle. Instead, I've carried it all these years. My silent witness to the crime.

His assault was a deep, jagged wound that scabbed over but never entirely healed. It festered inside me, roiling my sense of self. My emotional distress challenged every atom of my being—especially my future. I am logical and I am a planner. My new trauma-fear was neither of those things, popping up capriciously at will. Years later, when my gifted therapist wrote down PTSD on my insurance sheet, I had no idea what that meant, but I did know how it felt. Post-Traumatic Stress Disorder. Irrational anxiety, intrusive nightmares, tremendous shame.

I moved through the requisite horror of police, hospital, mug shots, line-ups, and more police, more line-ups benumbed. The distress I saw on my friends' faces broke me further. I felt my visible emotional pain hurt them. I tried to comfort them, instead of them comforting me. People whispered about me in the cafeteria. The police called me at all hours asking me to come down to the station. Days later, with no perpetrator apprehended, I declined further police involvement and left college. I flew home accompanied by a kind friend. I simply could not be alone. I went home to heal.

My folks were very caring and allowed me to remain quietly at home for months, making no demands on me. They loved me fiercely but were not equipped to help me recover from such a trauma. Neither my parents nor my siblings spoke to me about what happened. Reflecting the times, embarrassing family situations were to be buried and not discussed. Sexual assault did not happen to good girls or good families. Surely it must have been my own fault. It was an implicit stain on all of us.

Years later, my sisters and I were able to converse about what happened that night. In hindsight, none of us had the emotional language necessary to express our complicated feelings of horror and unease. Knowing the why of my family's denial of my humiliation and pain did little to help me recover my senses at the time of my attack. I was left adrift to move on stoically as best I could.

My life had been neatly sliced into before and after. Before was idyllic. After was hell. Before, I was going to be a famous journalist and writer. Early in my junior year at St. Louis University I had chanced upon a *TIME* magazine piece about competing alternative newspapers in Boston. I was bored with school, having backpacked through Europe the previous summer. My European experiences made me yearn for more adult living, outside my parochial dormitory. I instantly decided I was going to move there and write for one of them at the end of the school year. After—*my incident*—I couldn't possibly put myself out there, so exposed in a byline. Six months later, having no therapeutic guidance, I was still flailing to mend my shattered self. I clung to my pre-rape plans like a life raft and moved to Boston, despite having only two casual friends there. I realize now my actions made my challenging recovery even more difficult. I was carrying on through sheer force of will.

But I could never let myself succeed on the levels I had originally envisioned. Instead of writing for the *Boston Phoenix* (a breeding ground for famous journalistic careers) as I had hoped, I took a job as a lowly admin person. That would be a pattern I would repeat often. Entering the back door of situations, finagling to get close to the prize, but never quite allowing myself the prize. It took years for me to step through my fears and reach for what I wanted. My future successes were hard earned and came with a secret cost.

I endured years of terrified nights, convinced the rapist was going to find me and kill me. On my way home from visiting my Harvard pals, or hanging in a Cambridge blues club, I would scurry home on public transit to my cheap Back Bay walk-up with cortisol searing my body. Arriving safely, I would huddle in bed breathless and anxious. Later, after moving to the promised land of California, it would still rear its ugly little head. I would walk back to my car in foggy, misty North Beach on highest radar, prepared for the worst. The streets which earlier had been teeming and vibrant, now felt desolate and threatening. Even as late as the 2000s, when I would be out checking rock bands in clubs, I would walk to my car, keys defensively positioned in my hand, head on swivel alert, pulse pounding.

Remarkably, this traumatic ordeal did not destroy my innate sexuality. It dampened it for a few years, but there was no lasting damage. I never equated what happened to me with the sex. I never felt anything remotely sexual while the assault was happening. It was a power play, pure and simple. Rape is about control. Sex was simply the tool used to bludgeon my senses, destroy me emotionally, and hold me captive under his command.

For many years I beat myself up for *NOT LISTENING* to the voice inside that had screamed *DANGER. STOP. GO BACK.* Every hair on the back of my neck had stood up that night. Every atom of my being reverberated. The *Spirit* was blaring warnings like a trumpet in my ear. But I simply could not see the threat in front of me. This "nice" girl was unwilling to offend. That refusal has haunted me my entire life. As if I'm to blame for being on a campus street at eight o'clock on a Sunday night. As if I'm to blame for not wanting to give racial affront to a dark stranger. And for so many years after, instead of learning to listen to my instinct, I would freeze when I felt it nudging me insistently. I was unable to listen to it, while simultaneously unable to ignore it, caught in the slipstream of my trauma.

Healing came in various forms over great swaths of time. Self-help books. Kind boyfriends. Journaling. I muddled along trying to survive, while honoring my desire to live life to the fullest. I was determined to be with the most creative people of my generation and succeed. All the while, I was hiding my deepest self. Even when instinct broke through and led to positive outcomes (i.e., the Super Bowl ring,) for years I could not trust it.

It took meeting with the renown therapist and bestselling author (*Kitchen Table Wisdom, My Grandfather's Blessings*) Dr. Rachel Remen before I finally began to revisit and reconcile my trauma. Outwardly, I was riding high on the fame of the Starship band. Inwardly I was depressed and had nagging anxiety. I was still dating rummies too. I thought these ridiculous reasons to see a therapist but persevered. It took a few sessions before I even mentioned being raped in college. It was hidden that completely. Rachel spent many therapeutic sessions patiently convincing me I could do more than just survive whatever came my way. Her exquisite insight helped me realize instinct as a gift to be trusted and not feared. My emotional paralysis started to thaw as I learned how to better care for myself, instead of surviving whatever came along. I worked hard to define myself apart from the slur of rape victim.

Finally, haltingly, instinct changed from my enemy to my friend. Tentatively, I gave that little voice inside of me some trial shots. I left Jefferson Starship and started my own music business company. I found I could be successful on my own merits. Later, instinct made me go back and talk to a man at one of my music concerts who was unlike any other I had dated (he had a job, a car, and a condo). Honey's now my husband.

I entered the nineties infused with hard won confidence and verve. But I was still safely concealed by the greater recognition of my clients, whom I let define me. Although I had regularly garnered press for my activities, the focus was always on the event. I was always "Nadine from BMI (Broadcast Music)," "Nadine with Melissa Etheridge," "Nadine with Island Records." I would only allow my name to be in small print at the bottom of ads, never on top. Never.

It wasn't until I started my multi-day music festival, *Nadine's Wild Weekend*, that I realized the true depth of my psychic wound and the still-lingering extent of its damage. The irrational anxiety I had thought vanquished, was alive and well. While therapy had healed some wounds, remnants of fear lurked, waiting for opportune moments. As the start of the music festival came near, I found myself terrified of being seen, of being found out. Before, I always hid safely behind the scenes. But now, I was putting my name out there. *Nadine's Wild Weekend* music festival was all me.

I remember how fearful I was when my first full page news ad appeared in the *San Francisco Weekly*, a prominent cultural newspaper. I picked up a copy of the paper but could not bear to look at it. I drove instead to a church. Sitting alone in that empty worship space, midday, I kept reciting my fail-safe prayers like a mantra, "Hail Mary, full of grace. Hail Mary, full of grace." Over and over, I repeated them. Time passed until finally I could open the paper and scan the ad. *Nadine's Wild Weekend*. I had finally let myself be seen. Here I am. Here I am.

From the attack in college to that moment in church, time spanned almost thirty years. A generation. And though I continue to occasionally feel that familiar unease, I never again had the throat-closing, heart-wrenching moment of anguish I experienced in that pew. I realize now I spent as much time fighting against the past as I did fighting for my future. Clawing my way forward as if my life depended on it—because it did.

That crystalline moment in a hushed church allowed me to step through a door that I had shut forever— a lifetime ago. This singular experience enabled me to reset my outlook and eventually reorder my priorities. Ever after, my life would expand in increasingly positive ways. This was the lynchpin for all the transformational changes to come. Removing the burden of hidden, past trauma enabled me to explore other aspects of my life that I'd kept concealed. It gave me the opening necessary to reclaim a sense of faith. It allowed me to explore kinder fields of love and service. It emboldened me to dip a toe into hospice volunteering. It gave me the opening to embrace my vulnerability safely and consciously. It gave me the chance to trust myself, at last.

17

Nadine's Wild Weekend

I was standing on that hallowed altar—the stage of the historical Fillmore Auditorium. I looked out across a sea of happy, anticipatory faces, yelling my name. "Nayyyyyyydine." Nadeeeeeeeeeeeeeeeeen." Nadine's Wild Weekend was in full bloom. I was about to kick-off my raucous four-day celebration of San Francisco music played out in nightclubs and music venues across the City. The *Godmother of Rock* was in the house. Sweet!

I initiated my eponymous multi-day musical potpourri of San Francisco music in 1998 to highlight the long, continuing tradition of ground-breaking music in the Bay Area. A generation earlier I had arrived a naive but enthusiastic soul yearning to join those hip shaking, morality busting, psychedelic San Francisco rock stars. Five years later I was working with Jefferson Starship and laying the groundwork for my music business career. An additional number of years of consulting, promoting, managing, and producing burnished my track record further. After years of successful club concerts promoting up and coming young bands, I proclaimed myself the *Godmother of Rock*, a handy moniker for promoting my business while mentoring striving new bands. Now I wanted to use my talents to give back—a personal love letter to the city of my dreams.

The first year of my Nadine's Wild Weekend music festival, in 1998, featured "60 bands in 9 clubs over 3 days." It was a homegrown event, complete with my selling "all shows" VIP badges from the upstairs of a Mexican restaurant located in the heart of the entertainment district. Five years later it had morphed into "135 bands in 30 shows at 20 nightclubs over 4 days," with a roster of sponsors and co-workers. By the 2002 Weekend I was able to offer participating bands cross-promotional opportunities at radio stations, record stores and in print advertising. Part of my impetus was not to just showcase their talent to the music industry but also give bands marketing platforms to sell their records and raise their visibility to attract new fans.

The Wild Weekend was a huge, civic music party over four days. It took over every conceivable music venue in San Francisco. There would be five or six bands playing in each club, one after another, using rented professional stage gear. Each space had a location manager, and volunteers who wanted to be part of the fun. NWW had classic rock, new rock, hard rock, hair rock, indie rock, metal rock, blues rock, alternative rock, pop rock, singer-songwriters, electric and acoustic music, reflecting the broad spectrum of Bay Area music at the turn of the 21st century. I also created compilation CDs of the best songs submitted, that were sold at the venues to raise money for charities. The Wild Weekend was inclusive and open-hearted.

The event was enormous fun, and a substantial number of people gave their time and effort. I would careen from nightclub to nightclub with my riotous entourage in a humongous Humvee limo. I would make my entrance as the *Godmother* and say a few words of encouragement from the stage. I worked each venue carefully, welcoming fans, gladhanding music reps, and giving musicians short pep talks while I downed shots of alcohol. I genuinely appreciated the diverse local talent that participated. I had so many favorites; Oranger,

Mover, essence, the Locals, Viv, Vegas de Milo, the KGB, Michael Franti, Mermen, Ledenhed, P.C. Munoz, Beth Waters, Marginal Prophets, Chuck Prophet, Chris Von Sniedern, Blue Sky Roadster, Sunfur, Monica Pasquale, and Red Planet. Too many really, to keep listing, since over 300 bands played over four years.

I danced alongside fervent fans on beer-sodden dance floors. I applauded bands in smokey, filthy nightclubs that hadn't been cleaned in years, oblivious to everything but the music playing. Wild Weekend banners graced stages that were as small as postage stamps and as large as concert halls. I corralled the record labels of established bands, like Papa Roach, Third Eye Blind, Stroke 9 and Smashmouth, to support the weekend. Famous rock bassist Jason Newsted, who left metal kings Metallica to go his own way, debuted his new rock outfit, Echobrain.

It was an exhilarating and exhausting event. My feet would blister and bleed from walking excessively in high heels, night after night. My voice would get hoarse and croaky from unending conversations. My contact lenses would dry out from the smokey clubs and become unwearable. My personal phone never stopped ringing. Food was forgotten. By the time the Sunday shows finally came around I would be dressed down, limping around in flip flops, sporting eyeglasses. I would be so drained I would say yes to anything, out of fatigue. But it was a happy tiredness. It came from intense effort, winning collaborations, and mutual successes.

I was lionized in the Bay Area press, which proved flattering, overwhelming and humbling. Although I loved being in the spotlight, it took me some time to adjust to the sudden glare of attention. *Who was that woman they were talking about, anyway?* At that time, the Bay Area was home to six major newspapers (*SF Chronicle, SF Examiner, San Jose Mercury, Oakland Tribune, Contra Costa Times, Marin Independent Journal.*) There would be glowing features in every single one of them. Mayor Willie Brown gave me an official city proclamation. I was interviewed on television and the radio. Nadine's Wild Weekend made me somewhat of a minor league celebrity in a major league town. Bands fawned over me regularly too. I saw the hope and anticipation in their faces. I also saw the disappointment and dismissiveness when I did not live up to their expectations.

As I stood on that Fillmore stage, waiting for the teeming crowd to quiet, I took a moment to flash back to the bright-eyed neophyte I was in 1975. I marveled at where I had started and how far I had come. I allowed myself a private moment of deep satisfaction and appreciation. Because I knew, even then, other sirens were calling me. As unthinkable as leaving music was, I realized standing on that stage that Nadine's Wild Weekend wasn't a culmination, but a door to new beginnings.

It was now 2002 and other passions were coming into my life—passions that would eventually edge music out. Metamorphosis is never accomplished overnight but I was well into the process of change internally. Hospice volunteering was a growing commitment. It enabled me to reveal a different, softer side of my persona. As ridiculous as it sounds, I thought of becoming a nun early in my life. While religious life did not appeal to me, caring for others always drew me in. Spiritual concerns also began to take precedent, as I began to explore an adult understanding of God and faith more deeply. As I waited to address the expectant crowd on that magical stage, I instinctively felt this was the beginning of the end of my music career.

As I trace my personal trajectory over the history of the Wild Weekend, it makes perfect sense. After the success of the first year, I created a music business seminar to give struggling musicians basic information on how to break into the industry. I discovered I had a knack for teaching and traveled about presenting my seminar to music associations. After the 2002 festival, I authored a book for struggling musicians and creative types. It came out in 2003: *Hot Hits Cheap Demos (The Real World Guide to Music Business Success.)*. It synthesized everything I knew about the music business, along with behind-the-scenes stories about rock careers. I intended to go on a speaking tour after the book's publication, crisscrossing the country helping young musicians find their way to stardom. My vague outline was to produce Nadine's Wild Weekend in other cities, give a seminar, and sell my book, all at the same time.

Except... Life was nagging at me. Even after spending money on a promotional video for speaking appearances, I found I couldn't take the final steps to follow through on this initial plan. Something was holding me back. I skipped 2003, focusing on my book *Hot Hits Cheap Hits*, but faced a quandary producing the 2004 Wild Weekend. This singular event took so much work. Now that I was exploring other rewarding worlds, I wasn't sure how dedicated I could remain to music. I came close to hiring outside producers but ultimately could not cede control of "my" Wild Weekend. Did I have the will to commit to the additional years of demanding work necessary to become self-sustaining?

Technology was also taking over San Francisco with a vengeance. As mentioned earlier, popular music clubs were bought and turned into offices or condos, neighborhood after San Francisco neighborhood. Tech and streaming services were upending the music business too. Fast-moving changes in the industry and society would make record stores, CDs, terrestrial radio stations, and print newspapers irrelevant, closing some down permanently. Could I become tech savvy enough to ride the wave into music's uncharted future?

Maybe it was fear of success. Maybe it was fear of still-larger commitments. Or maybe it was the big life questions roiling my interior. Regardless, I felt hemmed in by Rock & Roll. I couldn't shake the feeling there was a better use for my talents than helping struggling musicians become rock stars. Hospice volunteering was teaching me about real needs. My lifelong love story with the music business started to fade as my abiding interest for the industry waned. The need to constantly maintain an aura of success within the music industry was exhausting. The music business felt more like an addictive habit than a creative endeavor. Yet it was all I had known for close to thirty years. I wasn't sure I knew how to leave it behind.

Music wasn't my only addictive habit. Underlying these mid-life questions was an even bigger challenge. My hidden secret. I was blacking out regularly after drinking. I had blacked out after both my Nadine's Wild Weekend regional shows in San Jose and Sacramento. No one thought my drinking was out of control except me. I knew I was treading a dangerous path hanging in nightclubs and touting a wild rock persona. But this was part of my image. Any band that saw me in a club knew to buy me a Budweiser and a shot of whiskey. How could I change by continuing to live professionally within the same routines that enabled my drinking problem? Drinking was a large part of my life with Honey too. How could I address the problem if I couldn't even voice it?

Those were the challenges I grappled with privately. Trusting my intuition, I was in a state of stasis for many months before my muddled future came into focus. I declined to produce the 2004 Wild Weekend, choosing instead to concentrate on my personal evolution. I quietly moved from hospice volunteer to hospice employee the fall of 2004 when the paid staff position as Volunteer Director became open. I advised struggling musicians (for a fee) over the phone by night while I worked hospice programs during the day. The more I committed to hospice, the less committed I was to music.

For two years I straddled both worlds. I wasn't comfortable leaving the music business until I had established myself fully in the hospice field as a recognized professional.

I needed that as my new identity. I finally cut the cord completely in 2006 when I set about researching and installing a new program of palliative care for my hospice non-profit company, Mission Hospice of San Mateo County. That program, *Transitions*, is still flourishing today.

Once I made the decision, I never looked back. I left music on my own terms, on top. Almost thirty years of life-changing adventures with creative musical talents gave me a rewarding, challenging, incredibly fun, professional career. I was glad to end my music career with the Wild Weekend and mentoring young bands. I had been there myself, all those years ago, wanting so desperately to be "in" with the cool music kids in the San Francisco music scene.

Having my own music festival showcase was the penultimate heady experience. No words will ever suffice to effectively express my joy and the emotional gratification over its success. In the big scheme of life, I was privileged to be another pilgrim on the path to finding themselves in that smoking cauldron of San Francisco history. With immense pride, I could finally admit: the *Godmother of Rock* had finally left the building.

PART FOUR

Love and Service

It was 1999 and I was still high in the music scene with Nadine's Wild Weekend. By what I thought was happenstance, I saw a tiny paragraph in our neighborhood paper. The short item advertised a meeting for anyone wishing to give their time volunteering with hospice patients. I marked the date. Stepping through lingering fears from my assault in college and producing my first Nadine's Wild Weekend music gave me new emotional daring. I was becoming much better attuned to my needs. Yet I still had an unreasonable dread of dying that I was tired of feeling. I had conquered other fears. I felt it was time to conquer this one. What better way to put my concerns to rest than seeing the end-of-life process up close and personal?

I had watched my Mother die with absolutely no understanding of the actual process. The same with my bestie JKR, who died of metastatic breast cancer. I tried to support her but had no real understanding of the needs of the terminally ill. I had no idea that palliative care (from the Latin "palliare" meaning to cloak or hide) meant treating physical troubles (pain, nausea, trouble breathing, diarrhea, constipation) through aggressive use of medications to maintain comfort. I had no idea that hospice considered both the terminally ill patient and their family in the "plan of care," because Mom's dying affects both her and you. I had no idea hospice was a team of professionals from multiple disciplines (doctor, nurse, social worker, home health aide, volunteer, chaplain) that worked behalf of both the patient and the family. And yes, I had no clue that Medicare mandated hospice volunteers to be part of the hospice team (because the first hospices in the United States were originally started by volunteers and the government wanted to continue that important legacy.) Like so many, I was woefully ignorant of the benefits hospice can provide during an emotionally and physically fraught time.

I drove to that first meeting, my hands white-knuckled, clenching the steering wheel. I was convinced the Spirit was leading me to a "death cult." Despite my trepidation, I could not ignore the intuitive pull to attend. Luckily, I found my jitters unwarranted. Mission Hospice was a small community nonprofit hospice full of smart, caring folks. I was immediately comfortable.

After that first meeting, I told my husband I had found "my people," surprising him.

It made sense though. One of the things I loved most about music was live performances. That moment of music and interaction between musician, instrument and attendees would never happen again in the exact same way. Hospice is not too different from live music. You know time on earth is limited, so you are intensely present with the client/patient. The immediacy and the vulnerability of both actions captivated me.

The open-hearted, kind nature of hospice work showed me another side of life. In the music business you were only as good as your last hit. But in hospice everyone counted. You could be as vulnerable as your patients in the pain, the sorrow, and the unknowable future. This was a revelation. End-of-life work touched a rich vein in me. Hospice activities reflected my natural, compassionate persona and gave my teaching abilities a chance to shine.

Thus, began my surprising second act. I started as a humble volunteer. By the time I retired seventeen years later, I had served as a Volunteer Director, PR Director, enabled and directed a volunteer palliative care program (Transitions), become a community educator, and a hospice educator working with hospital staffs. Toward the end of my hospice work, I joined a ground-breaking program of palliative and hospice dementia care, educating community members and medical professional about the needs of dementia patients. After retiring, I began volunteering with the homeless, still needing to give something to those less fortunate. What follows are reminiscent portraits of some indelible hospice experiences. I've also included encounters with a couple of homeless friends who affected me significantly.

Working with those in crisis, whether by illness or by economic circumstances, leveled the playing field of my life. You can't stand on accolades when people are at their most vulnerable. You can only ask for the grace to not turn away. Grace that allows the light of compassion to come in through the broken cracks of their current situation...

18

Meeting Mrs. A.

I'll never forget how the sweat started on my forehead, dampened my neck, and dripped under my arms. I stood before a nondescript door. Number 532 to be exact. I stood there nervous, fidgeting. I kept glancing down the hallway. Secretly I was hoping someone, or something, would come along and postpone, or somehow prevent me from my mission. My fear of the unknown was palatable and hung over me like a shroud. The lump in my throat threatened to gag me. What was I doing meeting my very first hospice patient as a newly minted hospice volunteer?

An eight-week series of classes gave me a crash course in the processes of dying, what to do, what was expected of me. It was an illuminating, powerful educational program covering multiple disciplines. In hospice work, volunteers are considered professional members of the interdisciplinary team of doctors, nurses, social workers, chaplains, and home health aides. Ostensibly, I was now a "professional" in the field of death and dying.

I surely didn't feel professional at this moment. I tried to remember my training. Examine how YOU are feeling and deal with YOUR feelings. My feelings were in a state of disorder. Turning around and walking away seemed a particularly good option. Then I felt ashamed of myself for feeling like such a baby. I had learned a saying in hospice, "When one door closes, another opens... but the hallway's a bitch." Well, guess what? I was in THAT hallway.

Shifting uncomfortably from foot to foot, I asked for the courage to be enough. I asked for the courage to walk in and say hello to a woman I'd never met. Mrs. A. She was ninety, bed-ridden and suffering from dementia. I knew she couldn't talk or feed herself or even turn over in bed. But what if she was a crazy woman ranting and frothing? My overactive imagination was starting to run away with me.

I slapped myself back mentally and toughened up my resolve by reminding myself that I could do this. If it's true there are no coincidences, then I was standing before this door for a purpose. My job was to walk through that door and care for this woman who needed me. That simple. That black and white. That immediate. Touching my hand to my heart, I took a deep breath of resolution. Putting the key in the lock, I turned and opened the door. I cautiously stepped into a nicely furnished studio apartment, with the bed hidden back in the sleeping alcove. It took me three or four tantalizing steps of suspense to turn the corner and see my patient.

And what a sight it was. A beautiful, aristocratic woman was sitting propped up in a standard hospital bed. She had a full head of impossibly thick, luscious white hair, stylishly done. More phenomenal were her clear, piercing blue eyes. They sur-veyed me coolly with equal amounts of curiosity, fear, wonder-ment, and blank detachment. She was a very living presence and that surprised me. She may have been physically helpless, but this was no powerless entity. Despite her near skeletal body, she retained an air of innate refinement. Oddly, I felt like an unworthy intruder who should kneel and beg admittance.

She was alone in the apartment of course, an anomaly in hospice. But her son had worked out a special arrangement. Her part time caretakers had left and would return later, to check up on her. The bedclothes were clean, her nightie fresh, the hospital rails up, the TV on. But alone. Totally alone, unmoving, silently picking at her sheet, waiting on an interior timetable.

I reached for her hand. Her grip was like a vise. She was unexpectedly strong, and quite unwilling to let go of me. I had to pry her fingers off. That was my first clue that she was not ready to let go and leave this world. She reminded me of someone whose world had gone completely askew, tilted out of control. It was like a dizzying ride at the county fair. You hold on with all your might. That was Mrs. A. Only her ride wouldn't end, and she couldn't get off. She was literally hanging on for dear life.

Peering closely, I looked at these remarkable hands holding mine. Her hands held none of the decay of the rest of her body. They were bulky in physical presence. Her fingers were exceptionally long and bony. For as strong as they were, they still held a fleshy softness. Her nails were hard and polished neatly. The palms, warm and moist, hummed with a different pulse. Her hands seem assured, vibrant, and held a certain ageless confidence. These impossibly elongated fingers wound around my hands in a tight wrap. I wanted to sculpt them.

As I sat next to her holding both her hands in mine, I thought how her hands so fully defined a life. They were a living testament to her soul. Holding Mrs. A's hands was like peeking into someone's secret life. I felt like a voyeur, but I couldn't NOT look. We stayed like that a long time. Hours really. My hands stayed wrapped around hers. We just touched and absorbed each other's presence. Waves of emotion would wash over us. I could not do anything but hold on and grip her firmly back.

Sitting with Mrs. A., our non-verbal visits were like a long Bob Dylan or Joni Mitchell song, filled with the quietude of poetic empathy and wordless soul talk. Other times I would try to read old-timey poems, or sing softly. She would moan in a fretful way so I would stop. She seemed to moan not so much from pain, but from some private distress I could only guess at. Her eyes wandered from fear and terror to wonder, reflecting an interior world visible only to her. It was obvious to me she was looking intently at something beyond my grasp of understanding. It took me weeks to get her to relax in my presence and let her eyes show me her true feelings. Then I saw relief, interest, pain, tenderness, and plain old, simple tiredness of living.

I feel this was my first real benediction. I left that day, three hours later, exhilarated, drained, and both more alive and more questioning than ever. My journey of shared vulnerability, unfiltered emotional connections, and acceptance of the unacceptable, had begun.

(This story was published in slightly different form in the American Journal of Hospice and Palliative Care Medicine, May/June 2005 issue.)

19

The Spoons

I had often heard people speak of certain other people as living in "diminished circumstances," but I never understood what that meant. Once a successful career woman who traveled extensively for pleasure, AB later lived in a humble, small space. I wrote about this in my journal, wrestling with the diminishing nature of life. I finally concluded that AB's outside appearances and circumstances were diminished, but not her person. AB was very much alive and vibrant. She showed me how a person can be reduced to a paltry existence but retain a powerful sense of self. This was a valuable lesson for me.

AB was one of my early hospice patients. Expecting to find an invalid, I was surprised when this gutsy little old bird of a woman greeted me warmly. At 81, she still had Oklahoma grit, an earthy sly humor. She didn't stand on ceremony. Despite being unable to breathe comfortably, and being almost sightless, she retained a healthy measure of self-reliance. She welcomed me heartily, too heartily—for I sensed an air of loneliness in that little room.

AB rested in the recliner. Since being diagnosed with terminal lung cancer, her shortness of breath had gotten progressively worse, and she used oxygen. Walking was now too difficult, so she used a wheelchair. She also suffered from macular degeneration, a severe eye disease. Her vision had been reduced to one large black spot. Lightness and darkness were discernible around the edges, but she could not visualize clear images.

Her room was tiny, with only a small refrigerator and a hot plate. A "Do Not Resuscitate" order was posted on the fridge door. Full bath. One small closet held her belongings. The kitchen had built-in cabinets above and below, which held her meager dishes and utensils. There was a single bed, her wheelchair, a recliner, one casual chair with cushion, and a low table and lamp. A television was on a stand near the bed, next to a reserve oxygen tank. There was a transistor radio on the side table, turned down low to the SF Giants baseball game. She was a lifelong fan. There was also a tape player for her books on tape. Windows on the north wall overlooked a municipal park.

AB had been a self-made woman. Finding herself a divorced single mom in 1920s Oklahoma, she fled with her young daughter to San Francisco in search of work. She lucked into admin work for the local bureau of a national news chain. She rose to office manager, retiring after forty years on the job. On the wall were photographs of her family members. A daughter lived close by and managed her affairs but remained emotionally distant. A handsome son lived in Colorado with his children. She adored her grandchildren and bemoaned the fact they lived out of state. She also lamented she could not clearly see her darling grandchildren's faces.

The only other item on display in the apartment was a wall rack of specially designed, enameled spoons from tourist destinations around the planet: The Alps, Grand Canyon, Florida, Paris, Rome. They were her most treasured possessions. After her kids were grown, she and a friend traveled around the world. Australia, Europe, the Caribbean, China. Her friend loved comfort, dressing up and socializing. AB had a stronger sense of curiosity and was less demanding of her accommodations. In respect for each other, they would divide the trips accordingly. For every trip to the Outback of Australia, there would be a trip to the George V in Paris. Each spoon represented a fond memory.

Despite her illness and disabilities, AB liked to get outside and do things. I quickly became accustomed to loading her up in the wheelchair and wheeling her downstairs and out of the building toward adventures. We went out every time I came to visit, which was weekly. Our San Mateo downtown was just a short distance from her door and was a lovely little community of shops and restaurants. We'd go to lunch in fancy and plain restaurants. She was never actually hungry, but simply enjoyed hearing conversations, traffic, and the bustle of everyday life.

My favorite times were when we wheeled through the downtown Central Park, which had beautiful winding paths. The children's playground was a favorite of hers. She couldn't see the children, but she could hear their squeals of delight. Her face would break into a wide smile as we sat there bathed in kiddie laughter. Those were sustaining moments, enjoying nature and children together, in the park's safe embrace.

As life moved inexorably on, AB inevitably deteriorated. As is normal in the dying process, her interest in current events, outside activities, and food diminished. She stopped wishing to go out, content to remain in her apartment. When she would go to her weekly hair appointment at the in-house salon, clumps would fall out during washing. More importantly though, she had become dreadfully fearful of falling. This fear was especially acute during the night, when she was alone and had to use the bathroom. She started having night terrors and panic attacks. Sometimes she stayed awake all night, afraid and fretful.

She began discussing options for more comprehensive care with my hospice organization. There were two alternatives: remaining in her apartment with hospice continuing and hiring a night-time attendant; or moving into a skilled nursing facility without hospice. At that time, you could not be in a nursing home and employ hospice services. Luckily for all of us, those restrictions no longer apply.

I went to see her, for what I clearly thought would be the last time in the apartment that had been her home for the past seven years. We talked only elliptically about her going into the nursing home. She said, "I wonder what will happen to my spoons?" I wondered too but lacked the confidence to know how to speak to that subject directly.

We gathered up our things and went out to the park. It was a picture postcard summer day. We sat in the sun and absorbed the healing warmth. For a moment, there was no future and no past, just a perfect present. We sat suspended in time, savoring the moment. I felt sure this would be the last time she would be in the park. I wanted to infuse her with the memory, the smells, and sounds that the park held. The children's distant voices were a soft lullaby. The sun baked our faces. Flowers scented the air. Birds sang.

Neither of us wanted to leave the bench where I had parked the wheelchair. Although it remained unspoken, we both knew things would never again be the same. She was making a significant transition in her life. It was only with great mutual reluctance that we finally headed back. We completed the trip home, through the lobby, up the elevators to her apartment, silently. She was still quiet when I gathered my things to leave. I told her I would be in touch, no matter where she went. I left her sitting in her recliner, lost in private thought.

The next day, she was moved into a nursing home, one that had an exceptionally good reputation. Good reputation or not, I was not prepared for what I encountered when I snuck over to see her several days later. I was breaking hospice rules since she was *off service*. There were too many old people tied in wheel-chairs sitting in the halls, staring vacantly. Initially, this was disconcerting and uncomfortable for me. I found AB's room. She had a huge bruise on her forehead. She had tried to get out of bed during the night to use the bathroom, but they had put the rails up on her bed. She was not used to rails and tried to climb over them and fell. Her worst nightmare. She was now confined to bed and in diapers. She had never worn diapers before. She felt terribly embarrassed. "I want to go home. Please help me go home," were her first words to me. It broke my heart, but I knew that was impossible. I sat with her as long as possible, buffeted by the sights, sounds, smells of the nursing home. I held her hand. I told her things would get better. I told her things would be okay. I didn't feel so positive inside, but what was I to say? I relied on my training to just be *present* with her.

Visiting the next week, I found AB out in the hall, tied to a wheelchair, all but unrecognizable to me. She had been given her morning shower and parked out in the hall, while they saw to the needs of the other patients. Her hair, still damp, was flat along her down-turned face. In that moment she looked utterly defeated to me.

Another day, I stopped in and found her very tired and distracted. She was wrapped up tight in her sheets, mummy-like. She didn't want anything. She really didn't want to visit. I stroked her brow and told her I loved her and was thinking of her. She was surprisingly forceful when she said to me, "Don't worry about a thing, Dear. Don't worry. Just don't worry." I had the strangest feeling that she was blessing me and saying good-bye.

Several days later, I again stopped to visit. The bed was empty and made up. I saw the daughter of the women who occupied the bed next to AB's. "Didn't they tell you? She died two days ago. She had a terrible time at the end but went quickly. I told them to call her family, but nobody came."

There was no funeral or service and I never saw the spoons again. I had truly little closure except the fact that we had shared a bit of life. And in the end, that proved to be enough for me. I've discovered that no matter how brief, it's these glimpses into someone's life that honors their living.

So often we rush by others, ignoring their existence. Before my hospice work, it was difficult for me to view misery and hardship in another's life. I was foolishly afraid it might taint my own existence. I judged people unfairly, sometimes meanly, for their circumstances.

I now realize acknowledging another's difficulty is a powerful grace shared between two souls. By not turning away, I lend empowerment and blessing to someone's journey and validate their existence. When we are called to be a witness, I think this is the witness the sacred texts talk about. Witnessing a life.

This is one of the most powerful gifts of hospice. Not turning away as someone's life ends. Reminding them they are still a special person, despite falling out of bed, soiling diapers, or losing control of their decisions. Validating their life has meaning to their very last breath.

20

Call to Service

As the Director of Volunteers at Mission Hospice of San Mateo, I was fortunate enough to initiate a pre-hospice palliative program. *Transitions* utilized volunteers to help clients who were hospice appropriate but still receiving treatments and not emotionally ready to stop. Volunteers would take them to medical appointments, run errands, help with groceries. If they saw the client failing, they would report to me, and I would call to discuss reassessing their end-of-life needs.

B was a client in this program. Fifty-five, white collared, B's job had transferred him to California less than a year earlier. They discovered his cancer only a few months after his arrival in the Golden State. He underwent tricky brain surgery, followed by an intense round of chemotherapy. He had just finished his final course of chemo when his doctors discovered a new, even larger brain tumor. A second surgery was only able to remove a portion of the new growth, and it left B terribly weak, in need of assistance.

His family lived back East and had no financial means to care for him. There was no money for live-in help or even part-time help. His sister called me crying, pleading for help. Truthfully, I had thought B too sick, beyond our poor little volunteer corps' abilities. I told his sister I would meet with him because he had no other/viable options.

When I met with him to assess whether our program would be a good fit, he was fresh out of the hospital. A large red, angry scar dominated his head, shaved for his recent, second surgery. A biggish guy, he was dreadfully fragile. He was truly perplexed by this life-changing, fast-moving turn of events. It was clear he needed greater care than simple transport and errands, but what alternatives were there? B was alone and sick. Extremely sick. And very, very alone. It was a devastating situation. I returned to my office, assigning a revolving team of volunteers to assist him as well as they could.

B was quiet with these kind helpers. They would drive him forty-five minutes down to the lauded research hospital where he received his radiation, but their efforts at conversation were rebuffed. He would answer in as few words as possible. They easily grasped the severity of his condition and how physically compromised he was. Without being asked, they would help him into the car, drive to the hospital, help him out of the car, into the hospital, go to park, then sit with him while he waited for his treatment. Post treatment, the routine would be reversed. They would retrieve their car from the lot, help him back into it, then assist him out of the car and walk him to the door of his apartment. But that was it. He wouldn't let them farther than the door. The door was the *boundary* line. No admittance.

After each visit, I would get these concerned calls from the volunteers alarmed at both his condition and his isolation. How could anyone endure this so stoically? I would call regularly checking up on him. Just as regularly B would slough off my concern, assuring me he was fine. The tone of his no-nonsense voice warning me to not delve deeper.

But of course, he wasn't okay. We all thought he should be in our full hospice program, ministered to by a team of specialists who could address his challenging issues and give him some emotional solace and physical comfort. But B had made it clear to his oncology doctor that he wanted to battle the cancer. Aggressive radiation to shrink his brain tumors remained his treatment plan.

I remained worried about B's safety living alone. He was a prime candidate for falls. Several times I had brought up the subject of a medical alert necklace. B would always promise to investigate that and never did. It finally dawned on me that he could not afford the monthly fee. He reluctantly confirmed this was the case.

I immediately arranged for him to receive the service gratis. Then I set up an appointment to meet the medical alert technicians at his apartment for the installation. When I arrived at the appointed time, the installers were already there. B looked terrible. Was the fact that he was admitting to needing this oversight? The fact that people were inside his apartment? Or was it simply because he was so extremely sick? Whatever the case, he had an anxiety attack, triggering nausea and breathing difficulties. The installers got nervous as B went downhill. They were technicians, not medical personnel. They quickly finished up their work, gave a cursory explanation of how the system worked and got the hell out of there.

As soon as the techs left, I assured B that we would just sit there together while we let this spell pass. His relief was palatable. We sat quietly, knee to knee, and I gave him time to recover. Slowly his labored breathing became less acute. He got some color back in his face. He relaxed a bit in his chair. I looked around the apartment and commented on several items. He loved traditional southern gospel music and had a large vinyl collection. He was a Navy man with appropriate Navy memorabilia. I made him laugh. He was rueful but fully alert.

Now that I was in the door, he could speak more honestly with me. We discussed elements of his current difficulties quite matter-of-factly. He was having increased difficulty breathing. His nights were fraught with panic attacks as he found himself gasping for breath. He was exhausted from not sleeping. He had no appetite. Exploring his apartment, I found a week's worth of Meals on Wheels in his fridge, untouched.

As I was working my way through my mental checklist, I asked him about showering, and he told me he couldn't shower. He was simply too weak to manage it. I asked him if he had a shower chair and he told me he did, but it didn't fit his bath. Before he could stop me, I jumped up to check out his bathroom.

Which is when I saw it.

Have you ever seen something that you absolutely do not want to see? Because you know it will demand a response that you don't want to offer? That was how I felt. I was childish enough to stop and pray to God to remove me from the scene, as if I could be magically transported to some safe haven. God answered me by giving me the strength to shake off my squeamishness and respond appropriately.

What caused my severe reaction was the condition of his bathroom. It was covered in poop. Everywhere. The floor. The toilet. The sink. The bathtub. The bath rugs. Towels. I peeked into his bedroom. It was on his bed. His bedspread. The carpet. His clothes. I'm not lying when I tell you I wanted to run away. Instead, I did what you too would have done. I calmly walked back into the living room and asked B where he kept his cleaning supplies. I told him it looked like he could use some help in the bathroom. No big deal. I had now been behind the curtain of his OZ and seen his vulnerability on full display.

I found B didn't have any cleaning supplies, so I went and bought gloves, cleaners, disinfectant sprays, sponges, paper towels and laundry soap. After I got the bathroom under control, I tackled the bedroom, changing the sheets, scrubbing carpeting, starting the laundry. I swore if it was the last thing I ever did for this man, I'd make sure he slept on clean sheets!

Later, after I had tucked his wheezing, coughing, pale body into a clean bed, in a clean bedroom, outside a clean bathroom, he tried to thank me. I sloughed off his thanks. I told him what I did was what he would do for me if the situations were reversed. I even joked that before he knew it, he'd be up and around, and over at my house doing my cleaning. Beautiful.

The earnestness of his reply was heartrending. He vigorously assured me, "Yes, Ma'am, I will be happy to come help you. Once I'm better." Yes, he certainly would. And trust him, God willing, he was going to beat "this thing" and get to that point where yes, he could help me! The feverishness of his belief was encouraging. This was the most animated I had seen B. It was quite amazing.

I looked at his broken body, his labored breathing and pallid face. If his doctor couldn't do it, then I certainly couldn't tell him the truth. But I absolutely knew there would be no beating this thing of his. I returned to my office thoroughly shaken. He was obviously much sicker than he had let on and needed more help than our volunteer program could safely provide at this point.

Even worse, in our candid conversation, B had revealed a vulnerability of hope that was shockingly intimate. It was too personal, viewing his deep, fervent wish to live. He had buried his hope so deeply, it was like seeing him naked and raw. I just didn't know how to digest such a private—unrealistic— reveal. My emotions were in tumult. Usually, my interactions with patients were highly structured and followed a normal, limited course. This was the first time I had been so physically and emotionally involved with a patient.

In a perfect world, I would have called his sister, his brother, his pastor, and his doctor and told all of them he was no longer capable of caring for himself and arrangements had to be made to put him in a more secure environment. However, I knew I was ethically and professionally bound to honor his desire for privacy and confidentiality. In hospice, we meet the patient where they are emotionally and respect their decisions. I put in a call to his oncology office. When I finally reached his nurse practitioner, I railed about his condition and living situation. She listened attentively, said they were going to see him in a week and would re-evaluate then.

I hung up discouraged and drained. Medical care, then as now, is fraught with cracks people fall through—all the time. I called his volunteers and discussed the situation. We created a new plan of care. Five days a week, someone would visit him, pick up the house, do the laundry and prepare food, if necessary. I would call him every day. Radiation was over but the rides to PT would continue if he desired. I called his pastor and suggested he visit B more often.

The following week, B's health declined precipitously. He was so weak he could barely manage to get out of bed. He had no appetite. Although he did manage to drag himself to physical therapy, the therapist took one look at him and told him to go home. He was white as a ghost. Whenever I called B, he would answer the phone with his Navy preciseness that belied his physical condition. There was something about the sound of my voice that reassured him. I knew he trusted me.

Finally, the day came for the long-awaited doctor's appointment. One of my most stalwart volunteers drove him to the appointment. B asked him to stay in the room with him while they ran some tests. The doctor came back in and said he had unwelcome news for B. There was internal bleeding, which is why he was so weak. The doctor told B he had to go into the hospital immediately for transfusions— No going back home to gather his belongings or gather his thoughts. He had to go immediately, and the doctor would arrange everything.

B, ever the optimist, asked what further treatment options lay ahead, after they stabilized his internal bleeding. The doctor told B there were no further treatment options. Nothing had worked. He hoped the blood transfusions would stabilize B and they could discuss plans from there. The doctor left the room.

In the retelling of this moment, the volunteer expressed how helpless he felt during this interchange. A silent witness to B's undesired twist of fate. He said B took it stoically, showing little emotion. They left to go to the hospital. After helping B get settled in, the volunteer went by B's home and got him some pajamas, his briefcase, his wallet, and other small personal items. Meanwhile B called his brother, his cousin, and his pastor to tell them of this latest development.

I called B at the hospital that evening. He answered in his by-now-familiar clipped, military voice. We spoke briefly. I said I would come by the next day. Was there anything we could do for him? He was appreciative of the call, but he had contacted everyone. When I visited the next day, B looked better. Replenishing his blood was bringing some color back and he felt better. He told me the doctor said he would receive transfusions throughout the weekend and be reassessed early in the week. All of us connected to his palliative case stopped in to see him that weekend. Kind friends from work, previously unengaged in his care, dropped off balloons and visited, after hearing he was hospitalized.

On Monday morning, B called me for the first time ever. He told me his doctor told him it was finally time for hospice. The blood transfusions were a stop gap measure and were already losing their effectiveness. Because B was a vet, he qualified for the hospice services provided by the VA hospital. The doctor had explained the VA would take over his care, and he would get a new doctor. He told B what a pleasure it had been collaborating with him and he was sorry it hadn't ended better. He wished B all the best. The last thing his oncologist did was arrange for ambulance transport the following morning. B asked if I would accompany him down to the VA hospice. My heart was in my throat as I assured him that, of course, I would go with him.

Next morning, I went to his hospital room. He had his battered briefcase with his meager personal items ready. A hairbrush. Family pictures. A book. Keys. His wallet. His Navy papers. He would travel in his pajamas. He didn't look well. His hair was awry, his skin saggy. He kept putting an oxygen mask up to his face trying to breathe.

The ambulance transport team came. They loaded B onto the gurney, I took his briefcase and off we went. I held his hand in the elevator and waited until he was loaded into the ambulance. Forty-five-minutes later we arrived at the VA hospital. All evidence showed B had a hellish ride. He looked panicked and could not catch his breath. Even the oxygen was not helping.

His deteriorating condition scared the ambulance transporters. The EMT guys wanted to get rid of him as soon as possible. The last thing they needed was what they thought would be a simple transport, to *up and croak* on their watch. They quickly got him checked into the hospice wing, got him into his new bed and departed posthaste.

The admitting nurse was lovely and experienced, but B could not get comfortable. He simply couldn't breathe. I knew he needed some strong but effective drugs to counteract that drowning sensation. Those same drugs would also help with his increasing anxiety. I also knew the admitting team would have to follow their procedures before he was going to get any pharmacological relief. It could be hours. His oncologist had not sent him down with any meds since he was going into a new system of care. This is a common failure in today's fractured systems of medical care

I kept reassuring him that he was safe. I helped the nurse set up a fan to blow on him, which might give him some modicum of relief. And I stayed and we held hands until he quieted down. Unfortunately, I had to get back to work, so I reluctantly left him.

We spoke briefly on the phone that night. With his last ounce of energy, he answered in his Navy voice. We talked for only a short while. He could only get the words out between gasps. I promised him I would come again the next day.

That night I tossed and turned thinking about B. I prayed for him continuously. When I saw him the next day, he was in a coma and the end was getting close. The hospital was keeping him comfortably sedated and had notified his family. I went in and let my gaze fall on B. For the first time in weeks, he looked calm, and was breathing easily. I stroked his brow and told him how lovely it was to know him. I thanked him repeatedly for the honor of being involved in his care. I told him not to be afraid. I prayed for him.

I went to work and waited. That night I remained edgy. I called the next morning and was told he had died at 7:00 am.

Could I come by and pick up his effects? The family was flying out and the mortuary was coming for the body. I had a long, contemplative drive down to pick up that old, dated briefcase that carried the remnants of this brave man's life. I cried and felt the loss.

I took his briefcase to his apartment and put it on his desk. I took one last, lingering look around the sparsely furnished space. It was the site of a significant spiritual realization for me. This epiphany would guide me over and over in the future. Humility. Kindness. Giving someone the gift of your time. I closed the door silently. B was gone.

B's death remains a momentous experience in my spiritual journey. B's illness challenged me to my very core. It was outside the bounds of my neatly prescribed hospice curriculum. Because he had *no one* and was so desperately sick, (everyone's worst nightmare), I could only follow the Golden Rule. *Do unto others as I would have them do unto you.* I saw the unvarnished face of hope in a hopeless situation and did not turn away. I saw a terrifying situation and rose to the occasion. I accompanied a stranger on his final journey and did not hesitate.

My personal heroes have always been those who answered the call of service without reservation. Jesus. Mother Teresa. President Jimmy Carter. John Lewis. Their humble ministrations to the less fortunate remain constant inspiration. Before B came onto our program, I wondered if I would ever have the courage to respond in like manner if the situation arose.

Being able to answer that call to service is *grace* in action.

21

Heartbreaking V

The relentless Arizona sun felt like a hammer beating on me as I walked across the concrete courtyard into the back building. But that was just my heart pounding. I had a new hospice job that required me to go into skilled nursing facilities to check on our clients. Despite years of working in the end-of-life domain, most of my work had been in homes. I did not eagerly anticipate this aspect/new line of work. I forced myself to open the door and was immediately hit by a wave of rank, offensive odors. I found myself staring down a narrow hallway littered with wheelchairs and gurneys.

I really didn't want to walk inside. I felt this resemblance to the fun house at the carnival, where every image is misshapen and twisted. Reluctantly, I squared my shoulders and walked into the crowded corridor, nodding hello to those residents who looked at me. At the far end, there was a herd of wheelchair-bound patients crammed around the nurse's station. I asked an aide where I could find my new patient, V.

The aide pointed to a woman bent so far forward that her head hung down touching her chest. Her face was hidden by a curtain of lank gray hair. She had one hand on the edge of her lap table, trying to pull herself out of the wheelchair. The other hand she kept hidden. I knelt on the floor next to her at eye level and tried to get her attention. For a full minute she ignored my insistent touch. Finally, she turned her face to me, her eyes unfocused and mouth agape with the remnants of old applesauce drooling out. Then her head fell on her chest again. It was like her neck was too weak to hold her head up. Irreverently, it made me think of a bobble head doll and I felt guilty for that insensitive thought.

I knelt there uncertain how to proceed. I wheeled her over to a side chair where I sat down and started talking to her gently. I rummaged around in my bag for the lavender lotion Rev. Linda had given me and attempted to put some on the top of her hands, but she didn't like it. Flummoxed, I wracked my brain for how we could have a meaningful visit.

The facility nurse must have sensed my frustration. Without looking up from her charting she suggested I take V outside for some fresh air. This seemed a better alternative than sitting there surrounded by a pack of smelly, sick patients. So, I unlocked the wheelchair brakes and carefully pushed her through the maze of bodies. I got both suspicious and jealous looks from her fellow residents as I wheeled her through this juggernaut of bodies.

When we got to the outside door, there was an alarm code to punch in. Across the hall from the code box was a 40ish-looking man lying on a gurney. He was missing quite a few teeth and his legs were in splints. I was trying not to stare at him while I punched in the appropriate numbers. I opened the door only to be met by a blaring alarm. I quickly shut the door, not wanting to draw attention to myself and V. The man on the gurney was giving me wild looks, eyebrows raised. He was waving his hands, trying to point to the keypad. I told him I thought I had the right code. He started raising his shoulders in a "I don't know but you should try it again" gesture. I tried it again. Same thing. Klaxons blaring. I looked at gurney man and started laughing. So, did he. Finally, on my third try, the door opened without incident. I gave "gurney man" a triumphant smile as I left the building, strangely satisfied by our encounter.

Now we were back in the hot courtyard, where the concrete was whitewashed by the midday sun. As I wheeled V slowly over to some shade, I noticed a small but notable change in her body language. Her hand was still grasping and pulling, but her head came up the tiniest bit as the stuffy breeze ruffled her hair. I parked us under an awning, so she was facing the courtyard. I had been continuing to talk softly to her and now I started humming. I relaxed a bit myself. It was an unusually sweltering day, and my blouse was sticking to my back. I ignored it.

It was peaceful outside. A few staff were on smoking breaks over under the pergola, but they didn't bother us. As she adjusted more to the still quiet and heat of the day that enveloped us, her head started coming off her chest for longer and longer periods of time. I idly thought about how tired her neck must be. Without thinking, I started massaging her neck and bony shoulders with the gentlest of touches. Her head came up higher. Then she started to lean back in her chair. After a bit of time, she leaned back into me, resting against my body, as I stroked her neck and rubbed her shoulders.

I found the more she leaned into me physically, the more I leaned into her emotionally. Somehow between my bumbling determination and the crumbling of her defenses, we both lost some of our fear. I found some Kleenex and wiped her mouth. Slowly, she put one, then both her hands on her chair table. Her hands stopped fidgeting. She was sitting up mostly straight and looking out. Her relief was palatable. So was mine.

I now was able to look at her more objectively. She seemed cleaner, and not actually decrepit. Or even that sick. Just a bit old and worn out. Another nice lady with dementia. I finally saw her normally, as a person with a life, a person with a past.

Maybe I had known her, or one of my sisters might have known her. Maybe she was a neighbor or a business friend, or a relative. She was someone. Not just a broken body surrounded by other broken bodies.

We sat quietly with puffs of stifling air buffeting us. It was so quiet you could almost hear the grass grow. And for a few moments, everything seemed alive. Death and sickness weren't omnipresent. The sky was blue. It was a sunny day. We were outside. Outside. She sighed— a sigh of contentment. Her sigh opened a flood of emotions inside of me. How little it took, really, to get to this place. Just a little time and resolve. I sat with my feelings, and she sat with hers.

After about thirty minutes the heat finally got to me. I told her we had to go in. She put her feet on the pavement and tried to stop the chair from being pushed forward. I slowly but forcefully continued our reluctant ride down the sidewalk to the facility door. With each foot traveled, her head dropped lower and lower. When we entered the facility, "gurney man" was still in the same place and gave me a look. I gave him a look back.

V put her foot down more forcefully here at the doorway, clearly not wanting to enter the building. But I had a schedule to keep. I had to return her to her home. With a heavy heart and a heavier soul, I parked her back at the nurse's station. She looked exactly how she had when I first saw her. Head on her chest, bent far forward, hands pulling at the lap table, hair covering her hidden face, mouth open, uncaring, defeated. I vowed to return.

When I saw her two weeks later, she was a small, curled mass on a mattress on the floor, dying alone while in a room with three other residents. Because of fall risks, and the recent ban on bedrails due to possible, unintended patient strangulation, all mattresses were on the floor for bedridden patients.

V was in a fetal position, breathing raggedly, unresponsive but not yet dead. She died just a few days later and the facility notified our hospice that she had passed.

Harsh endings like V's are heartbreaking. To ground myself in the vast mysteries of life and death, I learned how to reframe my view of those dying. Most people have a knee jerk avoidance to the dying, afraid they might see an unwanted future mirrored back to them. The superstition that dying is contagious, is also held by many in American society today.

I relate all this to the metaphor of magnificent roses fading at the end of a long, colorful bloom. I view the process of dying (and it is almost always a process, rarely sudden) as bouquets of curling petals, whose disappearing beauty elicits only the most wonderful memories. Like personalities, the perfume from wrinkled, dry roses continues to infuse a room long after their initial bloom. I envision these good souls as the beautiful, complicated, talented, flawed but loving people they once were, before illness crept in to rob them of their magnificence. I'm honored to be their observer, reassuring them by my simple presence of their eternal human value.

22

J's Corner

I keep returning over and over to J's "spot." The one under the freeway, off the industrial road. It was close enough for civilization (Circle K for cigs, coffee, and plastic food) yet far enough away from the family neighborhoods to not be hassled. He really liked it there, because it gave him privacy, shelter from the elements. And there was a fluorescent light under the overpass, so most nights he could read.

J was a reader. Voracious. He'd read anything you gave him, but he was partial to Stephen King. You'd see J sitting on his milk carton facing the sun, hunched over, and engrossed in a tattered paperback. Our homeless snowbird who migrated every winter from back East to the warmer climes of Phoenix.

Like many moments of grace, I met J by coincidence. I was driving along a busy suburban road and stopped at a red light. I looked over and saw an older man of indeterminate age, sitting at the corner, his belongings in a grocery cart, looking about as sad and lonely as I'd ever seen a person look. He had a desolate, haunted mien that troubled me. Two blocks later, I turned around and went back. I stopped the car at the busy intersection and shouted to him, asking if he wanted to get something to eat at the Denny's down the block. He said yes, and said he'd meet me there. Over a cheeseburger and fries, J told me his story.

J was of normal height and weight and seemed to be in his mid-fifties. He was from the Midwest and had done factory work most of his life. As an adult he had lived with his mom, his siblings being either scattered or dead. A sister had been close to them, but she died in a car accident. After her death, he and his mom got by. I got the distinct impression his mom was the lynchpin in his life. After she died, he just lost his way. "I worked in factories in Wisconsin, Michigan and Pennsylvania. Then after my sister died it was just me and Mom in Pennsylvania. Then after Mom died..." As his words petered out, he looked at me, his hands raised in surrender.

He was unable to manage the normal demands of living in society without her love and direction. I gathered he drifted around after losing her. Finally, when it got cold, he took a bus to Phoenix for the warm winter weather. It was clear he was still missing his mom; I have no idea how long it had been since she died.

He was quite the gentleman, even courtly, excusing himself to wash his hands before eating, using a napkin, and not eating until I started. Although he ordered a full meal, he could only eat a few bites. Being inside a restaurant, having hot food, telling his story overwhelmed him. He took most of his meal to go. I gave him a little money and drove away, touched by his dilemma.

Although, to J, there was no dilemma. He liked it. He hated the homeless shelters. They would *steal his belongings* and there was always the fear of violence in those places. He absolutely loved the sun and would extol its healing powers. Day in and day out, he would sit at the corner of a huge dusty undeveloped lot, traffic on the busy roadway racing by, facing our mostly omnipresent winter sun. He never, ever, turned his back to that golden orb. He said the sun was good for people and would keep them healthy and well. And it was true. Despite being out in the elements twenty-four hours a day, J was never sick.

I told some people about J, and they too started helping. He became our homeless guy. We'd look for him around Thanksgiving and say goodbye to him in May when he would return to his proverbial haunts back east. He would catch a truck ride or get on the bus and simply be gone, only to reappear with regularity the following November in his familiar spot.

This went on for six years, during which I would regularly drop off food, money, and paperbacks to him, as did others. Over the winter months, he would accumulate a better sleeping bag, an army blanket, and other small accoutrements to make his life easier. One year someone even gave him a battery powered space heater. He was always appreciative and grateful, but never expressed any real wants. J would always say he was doing simply fine and retreat into his own self-sufficient world.

Like all do-gooders, first, I went overboard. I pestered him with attention and over-visited, and he withdrew. I also tried to buy him nice new clothes, jeans, sweater, long sleeved turtleneck, and heavy socks for our cold desert nights. I never saw him in them. I assume he sold them or traded them. I learned to keep it simple with J. He was quite sensitive to over-kindness. He was a proud man. And he was homeless by choice, as he always reminded us. Even when it got wintry cold and drizzly, I'd check on him and he'd be huddled in his sleeping bag under the freeway overpass' florescent lights, hidden by the bushes, surviving as he knew how. No muss, no fuss. Our Arizona sun would eventually come out again and warm his upturned face.

The last year or two, J said folks were trying to help him get a subsidized apt. in DC. We often talked about social security and what benefits might be available. He would say he was trying to access those things. But they didn't seem pressing to him, and I learned to not belabor the point.

Finally, the time came when I couldn't find J. 2016. I drove past his old site, not really believing he was gone. He had become part of the fabric of my life. But alas, there was no sign of this good, decent man. No grocery cart, no bundle of belongings, no sleeping bag, no kicked around little igloo cooler, and as of the last year, no battery powered heater. I missed him. I worried about him. Was he somewhere else? Was he incapacitated? Was he dead? Only God knew.

After moving back to Northern California, I was back visiting my Phoenix family when my sister Mikki and I saw him pushing his grocery cart. I almost triggered a traffic accident in my haste to U-turn to see him. He greeted us as if no time had gone by. "How are you girls doing?" he asked, completely no-plussed. He recognized us immediately. He gave us no explanation where he had been. We immediately went to the used book store and got him paperbacks. J was back!

As of the spring of 2021, J was still in the neighborhood. He had moved off the busy intersection to a quiet, treed area back behind industrial buildings, where no one bothered him.

He now had a tent, a larger cooler, a heater, and a tarp for the ground besides his omnipresent grocery cart of detritus. When we last saw him, he asked us to run get him a bag of ice and cigarettes, peeling off money from a large bankroll of small bills. He may have been homeless, but at least he had money for necessities!

J never left trash. J never begged. J never asked anyone for anything. He was his own man. I admired that in him. Encountering him was a true blessing. He was my first, but not my last homeless pal. He single-handedly transformed my understanding of homelessness and the circumstances that precipitate and prolong it. Once again, I was back to the Golden Rule: *Treat Others as You Would Like Them to Treat You.*

23

Aladdin

I met Aladdin when he came through the homeless dining room for his third helping. He was a skinny dude with only a few teeth. His beard though, was neatly trimmed. He kept a cap on his head. He said he only ate once a day, so he liked to belly up at dinner. After the meal was over, I sat down with him to see how things were going in the newly sanctioned homeless camp.

The camp had been thrown together in two weeks. Tiny houses sat in long rows on an asphalt parking lot. Two fences, one wire, one wood privacy slats, surrounded the property. The small shelters were prefabricated and had been touted by the seller as revolutionary. It was a godsend to be able to offer these small homes to the unsheltered.

Aladdin was pessimistic about things at the camp, although in truth it had been erected in haste due to the local emergency of unsheltered people. It had not been opened long enough for all the kinks to be ironed out. The shelters themselves, were flimsy. The sides did not always meet flush to the roof. The roof often gaped on the sides. The doors did not always align properly. And most disappointing of all, the door locks sometimes didn't work. Aladdin estimated only one in four keys worked on the doors. He had some personal belongings stolen while he was there. It bummed him out. Money. Jewelry. Weed. He didn't feel much safer in the camp than when he was on the trail, although he was physically safer and now well fed. Although I knew all these matters would be fixed by the non-profit running the camp, I stayed quiet, sensing I needed to simply listen.

Aladdin was despondent and complaining. Life no longer held meaning for him. He had left home at the age of seven, as Allan. Now forty-six, his life had been one long struggle. He had found his sustenance in caring for others. He had become known in the various homeless camps for standing up for others less fortunate, less able to advocate for themselves. His homeless colleagues named him Aladdin —for making their wishes come true. A bike returned. A tent salvaged. Clothing returned to the rightful owner.

Now however, he had few friends and no one to call family, like he had at times in the past. Even more terrible, he had lost his darling dog, his soulmate, in an unprovoked pit bull attack. Tears streamed down his face as he recounted the horrible scene. His furry baby had died a bad death, whimpering, and crying. It only added to his existing PTSD.

Despite all this, Aladdin had an old soul. Sitting there, speaking with him, listening intently, forcing my mind not to wander, he revealed his beliefs: looking forward, helping, being honest, not complaining. "Turning OW into NOW," he said. He thought being of service was the best thing you could do for others. He usually couldn't help being optimistic. It was just his nature. Feeling so dejected was foreign to him. Realizing he had no future was hurting him emotionally. "Everyone needs something to look forward to. I have nothing. No family. No friends, No dog. No job." "Nothing here feeds my soul."

We sat for about twenty minutes. I just let him vent and talk. Homeless or not, how often do we really listen to each other? I was reminded again of how little it took to be kind. I told Aladdin how his neighbors were pulling for him and the camp. I told him he was important to me. I wanted things to work out for him. I patted him arm. I looked him in the eye.

When I stood to leave, he stood and put out a grizzled, calloused hand. I shook it firmly, not flinching at the dirt and grime. "What was your name again?" he asked me. After telling him, he said "Thank you for making me feel like I matter." "You do matter to me, my friend. I look forward to seeing you next time."

Unfortunately, Aladdin's hidden demons got the best of him, causing him to get into fights. He had to leave the supervised encampment. I later saw a photo of him on a homeless Facebook site, bedding down in a new park. The cycle continues.

PART FIVE

Love and Loss

There is something different about losing family members. The loss changes the orchestration of the universe. There is a large hole left by your loved one's departure. We all experience losing our parents, but the knowing doesn't make the permanency of the loss any easier to accept. Losing family members is as distressing as it is inevitable.

Like many of us, I did not grow up with any concept or familiarity with death and dying. Our grandparents lived away or died in nursing homes. The only deaths I experienced were those of beloved pets who were taken away to be put to sleep. With the momentous change of post war American families moving to suburbs and reducing family sizes, the multi-generational concept of family began to fall by the wayside. Without that mix of older generations, we were unintentionally denied the opportunity to see aging as natural; just like birthing is the natural beginning of life, the dying process is the necessary conclusion to life. Because of this, I, like many, had little understanding of the end of life and the processes that accompany the close of life.

My Mom suffered a heart attack and was hospitalized in June of 1983. Stressed by her illness, and possibly the thought of losing her, Dad dropped dead of a massive coronary while Mom was still in the hospital. It stunned everyone. Getting the news in my office at the Airplane Mansion, I was paralyzed by grief, unable to function. My kind friend MA (of Bad Boy Billy fame) packed me and took me to the airport. I had just seen my folks in May, when I was home for the Kentucky Derby and their anniversary. My family was literally hysterical with grief, my Mother still quite sick and perplexed how she had lost her husband of 47 years in the blink of an eye.

My father's death was a newsworthy event in Louisville. There were multiple rooms of flowers at the funeral, as for a head of state. Friends and business colleagues flew in from around the country. Comforting Dad's devastated older male friends shook me to my core. I had grown up with these men. They were the adults, not me. How could I give them solace when I was destroyed? Unable to accept the loss, I turned to even more drugs and excessive drinking to dull my pain. The entire summer after his passing, I hid my grief. I started snorting crystal meth daily. I lost fifty pounds in three months. I had reckless sex, with neither rhyme nor reason for my choices. Months and months went by before I could right myself properly. It was my first encounter with the misery of loss. Grief won in a smackdown. Later, I was ashamed with how I dealt with my father's passing.

It took the death of my Mom in 1991 to teach me important lessons I carry with me to this day, about how to help someone in the dying process. Although I knew nothing about disease, and hospice was years into my future, when Mom was at the end of her life, I vowed to be present throughout her journey, no matter how hard it might become. I was cognizant of my shortcomings after Dad's passing and was determined to be a better daughter for my Mother in her time of need. Still, I turned away from her predicament multiple times before I found the strength to face her impending passing with equanimity, grace, and loving acceptance. I will always be thankful I had a chance for a "do-over" after I acted so abysmally with Dad's death. I know you will relate to my story with Mom. While my account is long, it's simply my attempt to show how death is a slow progression of the body shutting down, not an "overnight" event that succumbs to our personal timelines…

24

Death of a Mom

It was a typical July evening in Louisville—hot and muggy. My skin and clothes were damp in the steamy night. I was back in Kentucky for my nephew's wedding. I expected my stay to be a fun, lighthearted trip since my family excelled at weddings. I hadn't been back since Christmas. I had no way of knowing this visit would give me some of my last good memories for a while.

I didn't understand my mother was in the initial stages of the dying process. In retrospect, the signs were unmistakable. She was moving at half-speed and had quit driving her car. As walking became an uncertain, laborious maneuver, she traversed through the house using each piece of furniture to steady herself. She was often short of breath, suffering from end-stage CHF, Congestive Heart Failure, a chronic disease. Her doctor told my brother it would be only a matter of months before her heart failed completely. We adult kids clung to denial.

Now that I was home, however, I could not ignore significant changes. My mother's remarkable ability to face social situations with ease began to desert her. Her emotions were uncharacteristically close to the surface. At the wedding's rehearsal dinner, she broke down, unable to finish her toast to her grandchildren. At the reception, after her friends had left, and the rock music picked up, she became uncomfortable, looking lost and bewildered. Spotting her across the crowded reception room appearing so ill at ease, I went over and offered to take her home. Although a dear friend would be performing at the reception, and I would miss that, my concern for my mother overrode all desire to remain at the party.

We shared a special closeness on that ride home. I'm her namesake, so our bond ran deep. We held hands across the console of her Mercedes, my fingertips resting lightly on the smooth flesh of her palm. Her hands were beautifully soft and warm. We laughed because I got turned around trying to leave the wedding reception. We were at such rich peace during that leisurely drive home. Deep peace. The greenery and lushness of the old oaks and maples eliciting nostalgia and comfort all at once. For that perfect moment, life was as simple as the sweet, evening air, and as constant as the sun rising and setting.

The rest of wedding weekend passed uneventfully. Yet I returned to the West Coast with mounting anxiety over Mom's declining health. She had begun living in the past increasingly, long ago events occupying her mind and dominating her conversations. It was difficult for family to get her to eat as she had no interest in food. She spent her days and nights feeling terribly anxious, fatigued, or both. At my brother's urging, Mom's brother and sister came to visit her in early September, in what was tacitly understood as the final goodbye, although I could not say that aloud.

I was both concerned and yet in denial. Living far away, I was not privy to viewing my mother's decline. I could only listen to family member's reports and try to decipher the severity of the situation. It might have been one thing for Uncle John and Aunt Flo to visit, but not one of my siblings was about to vocalize mother's imminent descent by suggesting that I come home. That would make her prognosis too real. But shortly after Mom's siblings visited, I too returned home, spurred by worry. When I told Mother I was coming, she was unexpectedly distant. She sounded preoccupied. In retrospect, she may have sensed I was coming to say goodbye.

Arriving home and seeing firsthand her failing health frightened me. She was much more physically compromised than when I had been there for the wedding. She had trouble doing nearly everything. I felt an alarming anxiety of Mother dying at any moment. I especially did not want to find her dead in bed, so the nights were excruciating. I would strain to hear any sounds from her bedroom that would reassure me she was still breathing. Then next morning, I would get up and wait apprehensively, until I heard her start to move around upstairs. My fears became nightmarish.

To distract the both of us, and because her hands were still lovely, I took her to get her nails done. Just being in the bustling salon overwhelmed and tired her. Later though, when I brought fresh flowers home for the dining room table, some old instinct reared its lovely head and she arranged them with her usual flair. Such moments were confusing and gave me unrealistic hope. She was not completely gone. She fiercely held on to her remaining abilities and independence. Even so, she was shrinking in size, and spirit, like a photograph slowly fading with age.

Because her personality had changed as her body was declining, she often seemed like a stranger to me. I found myself leery of being alone with her, so surrounded the two of us with siblings for lunch, dinner, and visits, careful to have no/little alone time with her. My siblings were more familiar with her new predilections, like pill-taking. She needed to take a battery of medications multiple times a day. Mental confusion meant it took her forever to take her pills. She would repeatedly pick them up and put them down again, in a drawn-out process of inspection, forgetfulness, distrust and eventual accommodation due to our nagging.

Where was the mother I knew and loved? Would she ever come back? Emotionally, I refused to accept the situation. I self-medicated myself to manage my rising hysteria. Per usual, alcohol, drugs, and distraction became my default. I reverted to responding like a self-centered adolescent with little spiritual awareness. My only awareness was of my own fears, not her needs.

The morning I was leaving, I wandered into her bedroom to see what was taking her so long. She was dressed, sitting on the edge of the bed, hunched over, looking fragile and defeated. She was weeping silently, her hands clenching a fold of tissues in a tight little grasp. I sat and put my arm around her impossibly narrow, bony shoulders, touching my head to hers. Her head fell to my shoulder. My mind was racing, alarmed that my mother, the strong matriarch, the bedrock of my existence, was weeping. I had never seen her cry. I desperately struggled to think of something appropriate to say.

Before I could speak, she spoke. She said how difficult it was to accept what was happening to her. In my discomfort with her emotional pain, all I could summon were empty platitudes and banal religious metaphors meant to comfort her. It didn't feel like enough. She finally pulled herself together, as she had done in the face of other adversity repeatedly. I was left feeling inept, small, useless.

When my sister arrived to take me to the airport, Mother and I had a clumsy goodbye. Reluctant to accept the finality of my leaving, Mother remained seated, would not get up to hug me. I knelt against her chair, my arms stretching to envelope her. The all of her. Her essence. Her being. Her soul. I couldn't get enough of her. I just couldn't. Kneeling there, my eyes brimming with tears, my throat constricted and dry, my arms wrapped around her and the chair, kissing her repeatedly, I knew I would never see her in that house again. My sister and I cried all the way to the airport.

Returning home, things changed profoundly for me. I was deeply ashamed of how I acted on my last visit—afraid, unhelpful, worried more about myself than my mother. My shame rattled me enough to take a few hesitant steps toward greater emotional maturity. I began to realize a few truths. If I couldn't save her, I could at least attempt to deal with these events honestly and without fear. Distance aided my intent. I no longer had to watch her progressive physical disintegration. I could hold a distorted but loving picture of her in my mind.

Almost immediately after I returned home, Mother had to enter the hospital. There was an alarming buildup of toxins in her body. Her failing body was now too impaired to circulate and cleanse her system effectively. This physical breakdown led to a type of mental breakdown. It seemed that as the physical walls crumbled, so did the mental ones. Old barriers collapsed and a lifetime of stoic silence, common to her generation, gave way to a review of her life and acknowledgement of deeply buried trials and tribulations.

Once home from her brief hospitalization, she began speaking aloud of events, activities, and choices she's made but never voiced or acknowledged. Mysteries, hidden thoughts, and questions surfaced in a torrent of wonderment, alarm, and actuated fact. Nothing was spared, not the stillbirth of her firstborn, her miscarriages, my assault in college, nor a sibling's diagnosis of epilepsy. Whatever had been bravely, silently borne in life was now open to review and discussion. Typically, she was hardest on herself, while I reassured her of her worth.

My family found her new volubility difficult. After a lifetime of following her lead and keeping family secrets carefully concealed, this latest version of Mom felt to some like a betrayal. It made them uncomfortable and embarrassed. While some in the family were trying to get her to shut up, I was trying to get her to talk. In fact, I tried to get her to talk more. When she was delusional and thought they were watching her through the television, I tried to calm her and soothe her ragged nerves. When she thought they were keeping her awake to study her, I asked her to speak of life as she knew it, the one reality I knew was true. We spoke constantly on the phone. Ragged, disjointed conversations that kept us both going.

I continued to call her night and day. The phone line was now our tenuous, fragile, and insubstantial link, pregnant with meaning and fraught with tension. I tried to save her from slipping further away. I scribbled notes of things I wanted to say. I thanked her for the little things, like how she always took the overcooked piece of meat, the dollop of veggies left, the burned steak. Little niceties that added up to a great Mom. I thanked her for big things. Basically, everything she gave me in life. I thanked her for her support and her belief in me. I tried to apologize for any thoughtlessness, or ingratitude on my part. I forgave her, when she thought she had been a bad mom, and reminded her of her great generosity of spirit. I reassured her of her value, the fullness and goodness of her life. I countered her every thrust of self-recrimination.

We spoke of our special relationship, and she told me how she had bonded with me at birth. We never had an argument our entire lives, except once, over marijuana. We talked about painting, art, and beauty. We spoke of love, and she blessed my boyfriend (who became my husband). She knew he was the man I'd been waiting for my whole life, a good, upright man.

She knew he would love me, protect me, and care for me. She wished us success, beauty, happiness, and love. I will never forget the gentle simplicity of her hopes for me. These clear, heartfelt exchanges temporarily helped overcome my turmoil in the situation.

Her life-remembered and her hopes for me became like the limbs on a tree. Some were dying and some were budding, but all coexisted on a single trunk. We were rooted, fused together in love and genetics, and for a moment, time stood still. Now when I spoke to her over the phone, I could almost feel her hand in mine. I could almost feel my arms around her. She was still my Mother, and she was still alive.

Because I'm a night owl and live on the west coast, I told her to call me in the middle of the night, when she would be most anxious and distraught. She tried one night, but I had just moved, and the new number was not on her speed dial. Her phone book was downstairs, and she was too weak to go down to find it. This made me incredibly sad. I felt personally responsible for the failure of her phone. The pressure of the inevitable finale was beginning to bear down on me. Her trembling voice and her labored breathing were impossible to ignore. I prepared myself for the end and prayed for a quick resolution. But it was not to come as quickly or as easily as I hoped.

The last week she lived in her house was deceptive. She seemed to take a wonderful turn for the better, to become almost her old self again. On Wednesday, she asked one of the home nurses to drive her to the beauty shop to get her hair cut and styled. She then returned home and went out to a favorite restaurant for lunch with one of my sisters.

She remained quite alert and called my brother with instructions to purchase matching emerald rings for all the daughters (and her daughter-in-law). She was extremely specific and detailed about the design she wanted. She bought birthday cards for impending family birthdays, and even went out for a birthday dinner with another of my sisters. This activity caused the family to breathe a very audible sigh of relief. Could we stave off the inevitable? Was Mother back? Unbeknownst to us, extremely ill persons often have a burst of energy before taking a bad turn. Which is what happened in this case. Before we knew it, she took a sharp turn for the worse.

By Friday, it was impossible for her to breathe. She was using a full tank of oxygen every night and frantically calling my brother each morning to refill it. When I called her on the phone, she spoke in a monotone. She sounded dull, lifeless, distracted, and unfocused.

On Sunday, while the family gathered at her house for brunch, old family friends stopped by to see her. The activity agitated her, and she became distressed. We didn't know that she was having an attack of congestive heart failure. Although she did not want to go back into the hospital, after some debate, they called the paramedics. Upon arrival, they immediately inserted a breathing tube down her throat and rushed her to the hospital and into the ICU.

By Monday night, her physical condition had stabilized but her mental state had not. She was now mad about being in the hospital and demanding to leave. She expressed her desires loudly, almost yelling. Obviously, the hospital was unwilling to release a heart attack patient from intensive care and so ignored her wishes. Mother was probably suffering from what I now recognize as ICU psychosis. Regardless, Mother decided to take matters into her own hands.

First, she took out all her intravenous tubes. Then she got up from her bed and walked out of her room, grabbing a bedpan as she left. Carrying the pan like a shield and dressed in her ridiculous hospital gown, she decided to leave of her own accord. She got as far as the automatic sliding doors at the main entrance before hospital personnel attempted to stop her. With a withering stare and threatening comments to not come near her, my mother froze them in their tracks.

After a three-hour stand-off with hospital personnel, my mother was transferred to another hospital.

When the family called me to report this latest incident, they were all paralyzed with shock, fear, and helplessness. Several of the nieces called me crying, begging me to come home. The situation was absurd, Fellini-esque. Mother's predicament was swinging way out of control, like a spinning top careening into furniture. Somehow, she had gone from heart attack victim to hospital terrorist in a mere twenty-four hours. I knew I had to go home and try to make sense out of this senselessness.

Tuesday night, exactly three weeks after my last tearful goodbye with my Mom, I boarded the plane for Kentucky. Unlike my earlier, fear-riddled visit, I now felt a sense of resolve and a possibility for personal redemption. Buoyed by our intimate long-distance conversations, I was now determined to help Mother die in peace, with grace and dignity, even in the hospital she wanted to leave.

It is Wednesday morning when I arrive back in Kentucky after a red eye from San Francisco. I will not let any of my family pick me up, preferring to rent a car. I am concentrating on facing my mother in the hospital room, and do not want the distraction of others' emotions. Despite my earlier resolve, I find myself dreading going to the hospital. I take care to dress nicely, even conservatively, putting on a silk blouse, belted slacks, and pumps. She always gently criticized my clothes or *costumes* as she called them. Ironically, at a time when it matters least, I want her to be most proud of me.

I pull into the boxy four-story hospital parking garage that I will come to know well. I walk through the hospital maze and finally find her room. Opening the door, I glimpse her before she sees me. She looks impossibly small and old in the hospital bed, an oxygen mask tight around her face. The moment she sees me, she starts talking and gesturing excitedly. Because of the mask, however, I can't understand a word she is saying. I sit on the hard bed and grab both her hands. Looking perplexed and pleading, her eyes search mine as the nurse finally removes her mask so she can speak.

The first thing she said was "My soul mate is here," telling the nurses I am the one with all the names, Mary, Mimi, Mary Nadine, Nadine. Her eyes became alive and clear, but it was obvious she was very, very tired. We held hands like that for the longest time, simply aware of each other's presence. The nurse left and I shut the door behind her, dampening the hall noise. The silence in the room was soothing. Mother's breathing was ragged and short. Wisps of breath. Grueling to watch.

I was desperate to do something, so I crawled into her bed. I held her like spoons, back to front. I tried to breathe with her. I tried to breathe life into her. She didn't seem comfortable with me in the bed, so I moved to the hard vinyl side chair while continuing to hold her hand. I started to withdraw my hand for a moment, but she wouldn't let go. "Don't leave," she said, "Don't go" she repeated. I stayed, and with the muffled sounds of hospital bustle safely on the other side of that closed door, watched her finally fall asleep.

Sitting next to her hospital bed, I felt a pure, cognizant connection with my mother. I can only call it Grace. Only when I thought she was safely asleep did I let go of her soft, supple hand and leave the room for a much-needed breather and cigarette. I was shaken by the intensity of our encounter and my sense of powerlessness. I walked out the hospital to the only smoking place available, the bunker-like parking garage. I reflected on what I had just experienced with my mother. Pure connection. In the space of a single moment, I felt my life had been validated. Grace indeed.

Twenty minutes later, when I returned to Mother, the room had turned into a war zone. My sisters had arrived to see if I had made it to the hospital. Right before they walked into Mother's room, Mother went into cardiac distress and all the alarms went off. The staff had coming running. Mother was frantically trying to breathe but also fighting with the nurses. They ushered us out of the room while trying to strap her arms down with restraints. In the puffs of a solitary cigarette, my soulful interlude had turned into a hospital nightmare. And although I stayed with her often until the end, seven days later, I never had that time of peaceful awareness with her again.

The rest of that day was long. Endless walks down the long corridor to the parking garage to smoke, then back again to the room to see if anything had changed. After the cardiac incident, Mother was kept drugged and restrained—since she had been belligerent to staff. It was heartbreaking seeing her in those restraints. Mother was yelling that she did not have a family, that we were all ingrates. The nurses were very mean to her. They yelled at her when she wouldn't do what they wanted. They yelled at us when we tried to intervene on her behalf. We siblings burst into tears in that hallway.

She wanted to leave the hospital and go home and made no bones about it. She was unkind to my sisters and said hurtful things—things difficult for them to forget. My brother and I were the only ones she spared, except for the nieces and nephews. They brought her a milkshake and a hamburger later, after things had calmed down, much to her delight. Although exhausted from the long afternoon, she rose to the occasion, calling them all by their family nicknames and making them feel special.

Later that evening I went out for drinks with one of my sisters and her boyfriend. He was a relatively new boyfriend, and she was trying to show him off to me. They were drinking and carousing around town as if nothing had happened earlier in the day. There was no talk about the hospital trauma or the bed restraints. I kept quiet about my sacred moment.

As the evening went on, I felt worse and worse about our distractive socializing. I missed Mother something horrible. I felt uncomfortable and wanted to be with Mom. I resolved to go back as soon as I could get away. Leaving them at midnight I sped through the deserted streets back to the hospital. I walked into my mother's room a bit inebriated and was shocked to find the chaplain sitting with her.

In retrospect, I can only imagine how I appeared to him, reeking of alcohol, wild-eyed and suspicious. Why was he there? Was my Mother dying right then? No, she had simply been anxious and had asked for him. He left to give us privacy and I turn to her.

She is crying because she wants to leave the hospital. I bring my beery face close to hers and promise her I will take her home, knowing this is a lie. Her breathing is terrible. I will not let go of her hand. I tell her she can let go and die. She tells me she does not want to die. She is obviously not ready. I do not know what to do. Finally, two hours later, I leave her room and stagger down into the hospital chapel. It is 4:00 a.m. and the chapel is deserted. Faux stained-glass windows and pews, cheap carpeting and an ersatz altar greet me.

I am crying again. The tears are streaming down my cheeks. I'm screaming at God, furious that He is letting Mother suffer. I smolder with anger. What kind of God is this? Where is His mercy? Let her go! Take her now! I do not care about sacrilege. I continue to rail against God at the same time scaring myself by how out of control I feel. I look around wildly for help. I spot a Bible sitting on a lectern and decide to read it. Maybe it will help me understand what is going on. It does not. There is no solace in those words for me that evening. I do not understand why this is happening. I finally leave. I have been up for 48 hours. I am spent, emotionally and physically. I drive home and go to sleep in her bed.

I sleep in late. The next afternoon, Thursday, I go back to the hospital, carrying a favorite cassette of calming music that had been helpful in the anxious weeks prior to her entering the hospital. She is pleased to see the tape. She tries to put it in her Walkman, her bony fingers shaking as she works the tape in. She seems relieved when she finally gets it inserted. Then it seems like too much of an effort. She lies back to listen but loses interest almost immediately. I am crushed.

My family is called to come to the hospital that night. She may be "going" so we gather to say good-by. She rallies, however, and it confuses us. Finally, frustrated by the lack of information we are being given, we demanded that a high-ranking doctor friend tell us what is going on with our mother.

I will never forget his description of her dying process. He said her life was like a spiral that would just get smaller and smaller, until it simply stopped. Like water down a drain. I did not really understand what he was saying. A spiral? My Mom's life is going down the proverbial drain? How rude. He did nothing to demystify the unfolding process of death. Regardless, it was clear she was going to die, and it was just a matter of time. He made it sound so simple. A simple spiral into death. No big deal. If only death were like that, without the accompanying physical realities and emotional heartbreak.

Our family is large. With the siblings, kids, in-laws, outlaws, exes and significant others, our number generally hovers in the low twenties. It was always difficult for hospital security because our numbers are so large. Our high-ranking doctor friend interceded with security, but even with his intervention, the way we were treated changed from shift to shift. Sometimes we were given our own private waiting room. Sometimes we were asked to leave. It was similar with the information we received about Mom. Depending on the shift, we would get information or not get information.

Mother was adamant that she did not want to be kept alive through extraordinary means and we had signed a Do Not Resuscitate (DNR) order on her behalf, so she could die as she wished. Only pain medication would be administered to offset her breathing difficulties and ease her along. At that time, in 1991, hospitals did not like patients who declined treatment. The staff shuffled Mom down to the end of the hall, the DNR order prominently taped to her door. There she was promptly ignored with only an occasional staff visit to her room. There was always a tinge of guilt now. We were the bad family, acceding to our Mother's wishes and letting her die. Of course, dying is a natural occurrence but still we were made to feel like second-class citizens, if not worse...*mother killers.*

Life is now centered around the hospital and trying to help Mother be more comfortable. I'm oblivious to the rest of world. I exist only for my Mother. Friday night I take her a milkshake. She's not really eating but seems so very thirsty. She insists on holding the milkshake herself and drinks a few sips hungrily. Then she calls for an aide to help her to the bathroom. It is a male aide. The fact that she lets him help her in this most private matter lets me know that her defenses are completely gone. But her insistence on getting up to use the facilities, instead of a bedpan or diaper, also speaks to her tough inner-strength. She's still not ready to go. She's still fighting. Why?

The next morning, I return with another milkshake. She's not as interested today. In the broad light of day, she looks ghastly. I leave and go to one sister's home, where we are all gathering to watch a special day of horse racing, a family tradition. I pick up a pint of bourbon on the way and start drinking again, watching the races. One of our siblings is actually at the racetrack that day, partaking in the festivities. In a news flash, we find out the great basketball star Magic Johnson has AIDS. At that time, AIDS seemed a death sentence. It feels like all news is sad news.

Around 7:00 p.m. we receive a call from the hospital that Mother is dying, and we should go down to say our goodbyes. We all meet at the hospital once again. This time it is different. Mother has slipped into a light coma. Her breathing is raspy, but she looks the most peaceful we have seen her in days. It's almost angelic in her room and we have a beautiful family scene. We promise to take care of each other; she doesn't have to worry. We each tell her how much we love her. We feel she can hear us. She squeezes my brother's hand slightly. We feel a sense of closure and peace. We go out to the waiting room, but the guard starts to hassle us about being too many people. Eventually we straggle out into the night.

I go back in the morning. She's not supposed to be alive, but she is. She's also awake again and so I try to make her comfortable. I help her sit up, but she's weak and tired She asks for a glass of water and insists on drinking it by herself. Her trembling hands hold the cup with shaky defiance, but the effort tires her out. While holding her hand, she says to me, "Your perfume is bothering me." I leave feeling distraught that I added to her discomfort. Those are the last words she spoke to me.

Later that night I go down again. Her breathing is labored and she's not speaking. I had found an old diary I had not known existed sitting on her desk in her bedroom. The writing is from her family's auto-camping trip in 1936 from Omaha to Los Angeles. I took it with me to the hospital and read it silently while holding her hand.

It's now Monday morning. I'm restless and feel pulled to the hospital. Spontaneously, I get dressed and drive down there. Surprisingly, two of my sisters are there too. We all felt the need to go to Mother. We walk in together. This time we know for sure. Mother is actively dying. She is completely comatose and unresponsive. Her beautiful hands are limp by her side. I wrap her hand around mine. I remember taking her to get her nails done just four weeks ago. Could this have happened so fast?

Her mouth is parched, and her lips cracked and dry. I put some lotion on them, and she smacks her lips. One eye is closed but the other eye is half-open, filmy, and sightless, mucous dripping out. She looks terrible. Really bad. Her legs are restless. A doctor comes in and tells us she is not there, but I don't listen. Her soul is still there. I can feel her. She's still fighting. Her breath comes in long wheezing segments with unbearable lengths of time before the next one. It's nerve-wracking and no one explains to me this type of breathing is normal at the end.

My sisters leave for their jobs. I remain at her bedside and hold her soft hand tightly, afraid each breath will be her last. I try to pray, all the while afraid to look at her because she is so ravaged physically. My fear remains voracious, and I am in the lowest depths of despair.

This becomes a pivotal moment in my life. As I sit there, broken and confused, I experience a spiritual awakening so profound it's like being in a dark cave and switching on a floodlight, illuminating new understanding of her passing and its larger significance. I truly feel Grace shining on me. I am fully transformed in this epiphanic moment.

Empowered by this revelation, I turn to look at this horrible-looking body lying on the bed beside me, my beloved Mom. With fresh eyes, I now see her timeless essence and unflagging spirit, not the ugliness of her decline. Now, I see her grace and strength. My fear vanishes. I can look death in the face. I do not have to turn away. It is now time for me to be there for her, like she was always there for me.

I move closer to the bed to reaffirm my new commitment to her, still holding her warm, yielding hand. I gaze out the window. It's November and the trees are barren. There is a cold, wintry afternoon light off in the distance. Looking at the stark grey sky, it dawns on me that this is death into birth. I can help her in this birth process. We are bonded in eternity, Mother, and me. *Yes, I will walk this path with you, Mother. You are not alone.*

I begin speaking to her, both aloud and silently. I speak of beauty, kindness, truth, love, and eternal life. I tell her she is beautiful; all I see is her great beauty. I tell her how wonderful it is going to be. I tell her she deserves the best and it is going to be fabulous. I tell her it is time for her to leave her tired old body and to let her spirit soar. I tell her I love her, and I thank her for everything she has given us, how she gave us everything we need to survive and now it's her time. I tell her not to be afraid, that she can let go, that I'll help her, and be there every step of the way. We sit like this for several uninterrupted hours, while I repeat my mantras of love and beauty over my Mother's failing body.

Finally, another of my sisters comes in and interrupts my soulful reverie. She takes one look at Mom and begins to talk as if Mother is not even there. "It's no wonder animals crawl away to die," she says, shaking her head at Mother's ruined body. While I know she's expressing her own emotional anguish, right then I'm furious at her insensitivity. I'm sure Mother can still hear, deep inside her coma. I hate my sister at that moment. I want to protect my mother from all negativities. I don't want to share her, even with my family.

Finally, it's Monday night, and I've calmed down. I've said everything I could say, and I feel Mother slipping away. The family has all gathered once again and we are taking turns quietly sitting with her. I am jealous of their time with her, but frankly I'm bone tired and I need their support. We cluster in the waiting room, crying and comforting one another. The guards have been unhappy about us staying after visiting hours and our large numbers. Slowly families begin to drift off home, in emotional exhaustion.

It's after midnight and I feel like I've been there for days. Still, I am determined to stay to her end. Abruptly, an intimidating new guard appears and starts yelling that we can't be there. "But our Mom is dying," we protest, while begging him to please leave us in peace with her. It turns ugly and he wins. I am forced to return to Mother's room to say goodbye for the last time, knowing I will not see Mother alive again. I kiss her with all my love, while seething inside.

I walk to the car in tears. I hate that bullying guard. I hate leaving Mother in that cold, incompetent hospital. I drive crazy fast, not caring now, crying, and yelling to the heavens. I turn on the classical music station and a majestic symphony is playing, with trumpets, drums, and soaring bombast. I turn it all the way up, screaming to Mother to hear the music. "Mother," I cry, "This music is for you, it can take you up to the sky and the heavens where you belong. This music is for your beautiful soul and your beautiful spirit. This is your guide to the heavens. Can you hear it? The heavens are announcing your arrival; can you hear the triumphant sounds?"

Finally, I arrive home, fatigued but wired. The guard had put me on edge and the house is cold and dark. I calm down enough to sit in Mother's favorite chair, drinking and reflecting. I notice for the first time, a lock box in the corner of the living room. It's overflowing with papers: bits, and pieces. I have been here a week and never noticed it. I take it up to my Mother's bedroom. I have continued sleeping in her bed because it makes me feel closer to her. I start going through the box. It is filled with important papers and mementos from her life. This must have been where her diary was kept. She must have been looking at these keepsakes before she went to the hospital.

I slowly start to go through the bits and pieces. I find her birth certificate, her piano recital program from 6th grade, her graduation diploma, newspaper clippings of family, deeds to old houses long past, pictures of Dad and her on trips, cards from us kids, poems, childish presents to parents, all kept carefully boxed through decades. I go through carefully and slowly, savoring every remembrance for her, reliving her life.

Then, I am stunned and stopped cold. I find love letters from her courtship with Dad. I never knew these existed. I hesitate, recognizing the intimacy. Love letters from my dad to my mom. Who knew? Whoever can imagine the bloom of their parents' love? As children, we only see the fruits of the relationship, never the soft tender desire and hope for the future. I slowly open the paper-thin letters from their disintegrating old envelopes.

I am astonished by the words and transfixed by one distinct paragraph. "Sugar, I would give anything to hold you in my arms and give those sweet, lovely lips just a soft kiss. It has been so long hasn't it?"

My Mother was on a family trip to see her sister in Washington, D.C., shortly after she and Dad began dating. He was writing telling her how much he missed her. Letter after letter of his love for her, and how much he missed her. Over and over, I read these stunning heartfelt lines.

"Sugar, I would give anything to hold you in my arms and give those sweet, lovely lips just a soft kiss. It has been so long, hasn't it?" "Mother" I shouted aloud, "Dad is waiting. Dad is waiting for you. He is reaching out his hand to you. Can you see him? He is right there. Dad is waiting for you Mom!" Finally, I fall asleep, my face tear stained, the letter clenched in my hand, under the pillow.

Tuesday morning, I wake up with a start. The letter is still in my hand and sunlight is streaming through the window. I sit up and look out. The day is a perfectly clear, bright morning. Mother's kind of morning. I look at the letter in my hand, as if I have never seen it before. Carefully, I start rereading those loving sentiments, softly crying now. "Sugar, I would give anything to hold you in my arms and give those sweet, lovely lips just a soft kiss. It has been so long, hasn't it?"

"...It has been so long hasn't it?" And then—I know she's gone. I look at the clock. It's 8:00 a.m. I look outside. I look at the letter. The phone rings shrilly, puncturing the moment. It's the hospital. She's gone.

25

Reconciling with Dad

Several years after my beloved father died, Mom and I finally discussed my rape assault. Even then, in halting, oblique sentences. Although Mom had been desperate to help me, Dad had prohibited her from discussing what he considered my shameful event. Driving back to Kentucky from Florida on the gorgeous Blue Ridge Parkway in the late '80s, we stopped at a motel to spend the night. I saw a man who unexpectedly frightened me when we were checking in. Typical PTSD. I asked Mom if we could change motels and she acquiesced immediately.

There must have been something in the timber of my voice that tipped Mom off. The next day, driving that gorgeous interstate thoroughfare, fifteen years after the attack, she finally asks about my wellbeing. I remember the juxtaposition of the beautiful geography with the regret I heard in her voice. She was deeply sorry she had not reached out to me. I suddenly grasped how this had weighed on her all these years. Yet, I was as uncomfortable as Mother was, speaking about this intimate violence. I hastily assured Mom that my therapist (who I was still seeing) was a tremendous help and that I was "healed." More accurately, I was in the process of healing over a vast swath of time, but I couldn't even admit that much. My emotional discomfort caused me to gloss over her sincere concern.

I wish now I hadn't been so afraid to reveal myself in that speeding gray Mercedes sedan. It was a vulnerable moment for both of us; long held pain hummed just below the surface. Today, I realize how she longed to take me in her arms when I arrived home broken and battered. I know now how she ached to comfort me, as only a mother can. She would have lulled me to sleep as she did in childhood, singing softly, her voice breathy and hushed, until I drifted off, blanketed by her love. In my self-centered pain, I couldn't contemplate her suffering— over not just the rape but also her own inability to help me as she wanted to.

Similarly, I had never blamed my father for his non-reaction to my rape, nor held it against him. I loved him unconditionally. He was a larger-than-life figure, and we all took our marching orders from him. Even after he died suddenly of a massive coronary in 1983 at the age of sixty-nine, his presence continued to cast long shadows over all our lives, well into our adulthoods.

Dad was imposing. He was six-feet-four-inches tall with dark, wavy hair that turned a handsome silver as he aged. He was gregarious to a fault, with a terrific sense of humor—genuinely popular. He was a successful, self-made insurance executive and a civic leader. He was an early supporter of the Kentucky Derby Festival and served as President and Chairman of the Board. He was on both the Louisville and Kentucky Boards of Education, along with the Louisville Public Library and Bellarmine University Boards, among others. He provided us with a life of enviable opportunities and riches. We wanted for nothing. Our family was the envy of many of our contemporaries.

Dad was the sun around which we all revolved. Swimming in the ocean during our month-long family vacations at the beach, he was the human raft we would cling to against the surf. We would be draped around his neck like monkeys while he stood tall against battering waves. When we were having family badminton or croquet tourneys, he was a ringleader, always making sure everyone got a turn. Whether he was quizzing us on state capitals around the dining table or beating us at Scrabble, he was always the patriarch.

Clearly, he was a man of his times and upbringing. In the 1950s and 1960s, men didn't show emotion; they simply continued silently. Challenging situations like sexual assault were meant to be endured quietly. If you didn't speak about it, then perhaps it didn't really happen. Unfortunately, my well-meaning parents lived by this credo. My family also lived by an established set of societal rules. I was expected to marry and have two children, exactly like my sisters. I had decided long before the rape not to follow that expected path. As I came of age in college, I felt hemmed-in by the narrow emotional constraints of my family. I wanted to feel and express emotions differently. I also wanted a bigger, broader, creative, worldly life outside the strictures of their society. But always, always, I was tethered to my Louisville family despite never living in that city again, post moving to California. My family was dynamic and fun, and I adored all of them. There was no place I'd rather be than with them on all the big holidays and special family events.

It was not until much, much later though, that Dad and I finally reconciled over my life-altering event and his refusal to address it. It was the mid-2000s and I was scribbling away in my little office nook, staring at the budding trees outside. I wrote in my journal about the rape for years, trying to make sense of it. I had a triptych of Dad and I on the bookshelf next to me. In the pictures I was a young girl, maybe ten. He is my larger-than-life Dad. Two photos were of us goofing around. But in the third, we are standing on the beach at our favorite vacation spot, Myrtle Beach, the scene of our most treasured family vacations. The two of us were standing on the sand, holding hands, our stances perfectly mirroring each other. One foot forward, one foot back, each looking at the camera guilelessly. Relaxed Daddy. And Daddy's little angel.

As I was scribbling about those long-ago events, I suddenly realized how awful it must have been for him when I was assaulted. In all my chronicling it had never dawned on me how the situation must have affected Dad. He could not protect me, his easygoing, happy-go-lucky, darling baby girl. He must have felt he had failed as a father. He must have felt he failed to protect me when I most needed protecting. At that moment, looking at him in that photograph, I had a lightning bolt of insight into his terrible personal despair. It was a stunning revelation, one that opened my emotional floodgates, allowed for the heartfelt acknowledgement long denied us. I silently apologized to him for not understanding earlier his deep suffering. His own deep pain. I told him it was okay, that I finally understood. I forgave him for not being there to help me heal.

Suddenly the picture from the triptych—the one of us on the beach—leapt out from its frame and flopped onto my desk. It literally flew out, alighting close to my journal. This happened without logical explanation. There was nothing physical in that room to make the picture leave its frame and land on my desk. No earthquake. No wind gusts. Nothing.

I knew then I was right. I wasn't the only one who had been injured by that horrible event. I knew God had granted me an indelible moment of clarity and forgiveness. I sat silently for lengthy minutes in communion with Dad, soul to soul. We apologized to each other. We forgave each other. We cried silently together. We comforted each other. We made peace. It remains one of my best memories of healing. Emotional resolution at last.

I feel fortunate to have arrived at an age when I can appreciate my parents more fully— for all their wonderful and not-so-wonderful qualities. It's a relief acknowledging their humanity without any qualifying of love or affection. Like every adult child, I didn't always agree with them, nor did I like how they managed certain aspects of their parenting. But I admire my parents tremendously and appreciate the innumerable gifts they bestowed on me. Gifts like social ease, conversational skills, critical thinking, love of reading, intellectual curiosity, a sense of responsibility, civic involvement, wit, wisdom, and a deep loyalty to family.

Age gives clarity. Even though I felt abandoned at the time of the attack perhaps their parenting gave me exactly what I needed to survive and succeed: steely inner strength and gutsy determination to overcome any obstacle. Love is love is love is love. Thank you Richard B. and Nadine Wrabetz Condon. You are still my heroes.

26

Our Beautiful Kathleen

My gorgeous sister Kathi Wade was dying. All seventy-five pounds of her in that small single bed. Her faithful dog KayCee was on the bed too, unwilling to leave her side. Although I had been a hospice professional for seventeen years, my objectivity flew out the window when her son told me she was entering hospice. In my anguished state over losing her, I was in denial of her condition, despite hearing all reports to the contrary. Deep down I couldn't believe my beautiful, capable sister was finally dying, after twenty years struggling with Parkinson's Disease. I was bereft emotionally for weeks, trying to come to terms.

Kathi had been the belle of the ball in our family. Beautiful blue eyes, blond hair, trim frame, she was the outlier. Most of us are tall and big, like our Dad. Kathi was shorter, only 5'7", the ballerina, the princess, the one always perfectly coiffed and dressed to the nines, while the rest of us wrestled with hair and inept fashion sense. Kathi was the life of any party, be it family or friends. She kept up with the latest fashion and cultural trends and was a natural ringleader. She loved to socialize and was routinely the most popular girl in any setting. Her entire life, men fell over themselves wanting to date her, be close to her, or bask in her extended glow. Like our Mother, she had that special knack of putting everyone at ease.

After finally arriving at her bedside from out of town, and observing her dying process in full flower, my hospice training finally kicked in. I accepted the inevitable and settled down to assist her in her transition. She was comatose, but I knew my voice and presence would still comfort her. Although her remarkable beauty was long gone and gauntness had stretched her face tight, her forehead still looked smooth and surprisingly young. I could brush her skeletal brow with my fingertips every so lightly and murmur sweet nothings. I would curl my fingers around her emaciated fingers and talk to her softly, laughing at our memories, and crying too. I'd play Leon Russell or Bob Dylan on my phone. I'd recall our myriad musical adventures together. Music had always been our touchstone. Two concert memories crowded my heart as I quietly sat with her.

The first was when we conspired to meet our hero, Leon Russell, backstage in Lexington, Kentucky. The year was 1974. Kathi was nine years older than me. I had idolized her growing up but didn't know her. She spent her high school in boarding school, went away to college, then wed after graduation and had two children. After my stint in Boston, I returned home to Louisville to save money for my move to San Francisco. Even though she was married with two young children, her marriage was crumbling. She too, was caught up in the rock and roaring feminist 1970s, wanting more from her life. She would routinely give her paycheck from teaching grade school to her husband, who would then give her an allowance. This floored me. While Kathi loved her darling children fiercely, like many women her age, she felt stifled in the mother-housewife role. I was no help in this regard, dismissive of children and the married lifestyle, although I was crazy about my nephews and nieces.

After connecting as adults for the first time, we bonded emotionally over Rock & Roll music. I invited her to join my group of local college friends, whenever she could get away. We were a loose coed gang, who smoked dope, played all the current records, went to music bars, concerts and got into heated debates about the Grateful Dead and ZZ Top. Kathi would show up in her tennis outfit, coming straight from her country club, to join us. We made quite the pair. I had the hippie cred, and she had the beauty cred.

By May of 1974, Leon Russell was a bona fide rock icon in our book, and we cooked up a scheme to meet him. We contacted Leon's management under the pretense of asking Leon to play an event celebrating the Kentucky Derby Festival. Our family was long involved with the festivities, so we didn't think stretching the truth a mile or two mattered. In fact, we drove to the concert in our Kentucky Derby Festival *hospitality* car, a snazzy white Cadillac convertible emblazoned with the festival's "Flying Pegasus" logo on the doors. Somewhere in our subconscious, we were hoping we could *kidnap* Leon and drive him around, while playing Little Richard in the 8-track. This was our favorite activity with the local musicians we admired in local clubs, driving them around blasting Little Richard. Kathi was a Little Richard fanatic and knew his songs by heart. *"Wop bop a loo bop a lop bom bom!"* Little Richard's galvanizing Rock & Roll clarion call fueled our nights.

I was in full hippy regalia, wearing one of my costumes. Untamed natural hair, lavender glasses, a crop top featuring a glittering butterfly over the boobs, and long jean skirt with glittering inserts. I was crowned with a custom leather hat, complete with secret stash pouch for my illegal weed. My sister Kathi, true to form, was wearing chic clothes of the latest style, charmingly sophisticated and glamorous. She could have stepped out of the trendiest Hollywood nightclub. Her beauty was the first thing anyone noticed. Always.

Backstage was decidedly a let-down. A spare room with folding chairs and a motley crew waited with us. When Leon entered the room, we all fell silent with awe. His was a perfunctory visit. He expressed zero interest in us or the Kentucky Derby. Even more surprisingly, he is the only man I've ever known who did not respond to my sister Kathi's beauty. It floored both of us. He spent all his time in that tacky backstage room talking to a disabled girl in a wheelchair. We were both mildly perturbed that he didn't see how hip we were—not the kindly disabled fan. I was still very naïve and self-centered. Kathi was simply unused to rejection. Quickly enough it was time for him to perform and he left the meet and greet room to walk to the arena.

The memory reminds utterly vivid in my mind. The darkened hallway leading to the stage became church-like, wide, and quiet, the noise from the arena crowd muffled, distant. Leon walked alone, silently—each bandy-legged step slow and deliberate. He was trailed off to one side and behind by his road manager, a protective presence, who ushered him to the stage like a dutiful, watchful herding dog. As I watched his receding back, his long mane of silvery hair cascading down his shirt, I saw Leon tensing up and turning inward. I saw him gather into himself, an actual physical metamorphous. He didn't get taller. He got harder, tighter, compressed, like a diamond. The private Leon and the public Leon. It was my first taste of *star power* and what sets certain artists apart. The aura of a superstar. The only people I ever saw with that same presence were the incredible Grace Slick and the football great Marcus Allen—but those are stories for other chapters. As I stood transfixed, I knew I had just seen something incredible. That image of Leon has never left me and might have become an unconscious impetus for my move to California to dive into Rock & Roll.

While Kathleen slept, a second memory of us together kept weirdly pushing into my consciousness, even though it didn't make sense to me. It was the time we saw the singer-songwriter Jimmy Jones—again in 1974, during our rockin' Louisville years. Kathi had been an aficionado of race records from her teenage years, though that was before my time. Jones' recordings of "Handy Man" and "Good Timing" sold millions of singles 45s in the 1950s and were later covered by artists like James Taylor. At that time, though, Jones was simply another *has been*. We saw him in a scuzzy club in the equally decrepit Mid-City Mall. The bar had a miniscule stage and a cheap sound system. Kathi pointed out how he "cupped his mic, trying to get every sound, a sign of the inferior quality of the equipment." I was so impressed that she knew that. This was another example of how worldly and knowledgeable my sister always seemed to me.

It was my first glimpse of how far you could fall in the entertainment business. Both those songs had been million sellers in the not distant past 50s. Jimmy went through the motions perfunctorily, another shocking peek into the music business. It was a paycheck for him, his celebrity and money long gone. The crowd was scant, and we were frankly embarrassed to be at such a loser show. But we hooted and hollered anyway when he played the hits. Even in this sad scene, the magic of the music still rang true, even in fluttering, tattered nostalgia. It was my first but not my last understanding of the cruelty of fame.

I can't tell you why those two memories kept crowding my brain as I stayed with her that final night. It had been over forty years with a lot of life lived in between. We had enjoyed wilder times and met more than our share of entertainers after I entered the music business. Our lives had veered off in different directions. Truth be told, we had not always been so comfortable with each other's life choices. Kathi was not a saint, and neither was I. We each made some poor decisions, some personal mistakes. But we remained closely tethered regardless.

In later years, she found me too goody-goody. I found her too concerned with appearances. Yet, we found new intimacy as her disease progressed, stripping us both of artifice. Parkinson's erased her beauty, then her independence. As her world compressed, it morphed into weekend shopping trips to Walgreens, simply to get her out. While these music memories seemed anachronistic to our current lives, they continued to bind us. I puzzled why these two instances from long ago were forefront and present in my mind. Was it the fact that we were so youthful, most of life in front of us, in 1974? Here we were, decades later, life draining from one of us, a heart breaking in the other.

Life reviews have their own twisted logic. This one highlighted much that characterized our relationship—our lifelong connection, our wonderful, shared experiences, the admiration I always felt for her and the awe I held her in most of my life. Despite multitudinous family, Kathi would be my final touchstone of family of a certain age, and of our charmed youth, our generous parents, our dearest family memories. She was the embodiment of class, just like our folks. Like Mom, she was a superb hostess and conversationalist; she was always beautifully dressed, made up and styled. Like Dad, she never met a stranger, charming everyone she met; she too became a successful, respected executive, managing a busy and highly regarded University of Louisville medical clinic, while serving on several University Boards.

Kathi maintained our family traditions after the folks died. She adhered to Dad's resolute Irish mantra of family. Whereas we might play family volleyball in the olden days with the folks, as we siblings became the eldest generation, Kathi insisted on charades or card games. It was hard to have a family gathering without it devolving into some parlor game of pitiless competition and braying laughter from the peanut gallery. Kathi was a natural instigator, her Christmases unforgettable, her enthusiasms irresistible.

As I watched her labored breathing, the breaths coming farther and farther apart, all I could do was sit and wonder at the immensity of it all. The immense hole her death would leave. The blessing that it was. I tried to simply be with her and absorb the moment completely. I refused to look away. I insisted on seeing only her beauty, right to the end. This was my final gift to my sister, my confidant, and my last link to our golden youth.

• • •   • • •   • • •

I'd be remiss to not mention my oldest sister Linda Donaldson (1939-2001), and my youngest sibling, Rick Condon Jr. (1955-2021). Both died of surgical errors that led to their premature deaths. I miss Linda's dry, quicksilver wit and smart quips. She was so funny one of our nieces thought she went to comedy school. There was simply no one that didn't love Linda, who was also my godmother. Rick and I had a lifelong, special connection. Like everyone in the family, he had a terrific sense of humor, especially for puns. He was a stellar teacher, had a sense of civic duty, and was a champion trivia player. He was the only boy, after five girls. I miss all of them dearly.

PART SIX

Unholy Faith

It's tricky to talk about faith. It's as personal as your DNA. I believe whole-heartedly in God but have spent much of my life shying away from discussing it publicly. Often, I was afraid of being singled out as "uncool." But it's also because my beliefs have changed and mutated so greatly over the course of my existence. You don't need a religion to need to connect with life's greater meanings. In fact, many of my greatest teachers have no structured religion at all.

For me, spirituality is an exploration that will not end until my very last breath. I find meaning to be a tumultuous journey of blasphemy, joy, sweat, tears, doubt, mystery, anger, and awe. I find the vulnerability of spiritual awareness to be bracing in our rough and tumble world. What follows is an attempt to artic-ulate my spiritual adventures in a manner that inspires you to explore your own connection to this universe…

27

Rebel Girl

I had the good fortune to backpack across Europe in the summer of 1971, before my junior year of college, and after that momentous evening in Big Sur at the Esalen baths. At twenty, I was footloose and fancy free, multi-tasking at coming of age. I had ditched my girlfriends, although I didn't reveal this fact to my parents. I had a Eurail train pass and flitted about Europe alone, as my whims dictated. I was reading both Jerry Rubin's Yippie manifesto *Steal This Book* and George Orwell's *Down and Out in Paris and London*. I was singing Dylan's *"Like a Rolling Stone"* with the other young backpackers that flooded Europe that summer. *"How does it feel, to be on your own, with no direction home, a complete unknown,"* Dylan sang.

It felt great in my case, thousands of miles away from my conventional upbringing, cautiously exploring my nascent sexuality. I fell into a brief but loving triad experience with two darling men I had met on the Spanish Steps in Rome. It was more liberating than sexual, Steve, Ennio and I smoking hashish in that tiny garret apartment, all of us companionably naked while overlooking the patchwork of Roman roofs. Miraculously I ran into my bestie JK in Rome. She was at the bottom of the Spanish Steps, and I was at the top. She joined us in taking the newly built subway system to see the rock band Pink Floyd on the outskirts of Rome. We missed the last train back into town. We spent the night sitting in a closed outdoor café, taking small hits of speed, and talking our asses off in three languages. It was against this backdrop of my changing personal mores that I went to see the Vatican, the seat of the Catholic Church.

My religious background was a typical one for the times. I was raised in an Irish Catholic family and educated at female Catholic schools by Ursuline nuns. I didn't share a classroom with a boy until college. In grade school, I was a pious girl who thought of becoming a nun. My faith was defined by guardian angels, a benevolent God, the Father, a crucified Son, Jesus, and an indefinable phenomenon called the "Holy Ghost." The Catholic ritual of mass, seeming interminable at times, had extraordinarily little meaning to me. The 1950s Catholic Church (as now) was a bigoted bastion of male authoritarianism and tradition, conducted in an ancient language (Latin).

High school saw a notable change in my religious education. In response to the inceptive changes of Vatican II, the nuns challenged us to redefine faith more maturely. We read Kierkegaard and discussed no man being an island. We listened to Simon and Garfunkel, "I Am a Rock," and the Beatles, "Blackbird," in religion classes. Our hootenannies at a popular teen gathering spot, Hogan's Fountain, were folk/gospel songs, "Michael Row the Boat Ashore" and "If I had a Hammer." We became bolder in our thinking, just as the Catholic Church became bolder by turning the altar around, translating the Mass into English and otherwise upsetting the older generations.

This boldness in thinking matched the tumult of our times. Free love was gaining a foothold and authority was being questioned. Americans were protesting the Vietnam War. Women's liberation was in its infancy. By the time we were seniors, we started sleeping with our boyfriends while making college plans. Rebelling against sexual mores was the first rent in our Catholic childhood belief systems. But honestly, the church, sex and I were never a good fit. I have never believed sex was wrong, or a sin, then or now.

College certainly finished tearing that curtain asunder. Although I attended two Jesuit Universities, religion now had little place in my life. The intention of Mass as community was replaced with the community of music, marijuana, and politics. Modern youth culture had a decidedly "us" versus "them" aspect to it. My tribe was easily identifiable---jeans and joints. We marched against the Vietnam War and for Earth Day. We closed Marquette University after the Kent State killings. The next year, I transferred to St. Louis University for my boyfriend. We promptly broke up and I had my first experience with marijuana. I led a protest for co-ed student housing and spearheaded opening a co-op store on campus. My new college pals and I traveled extensively together in VW vans across the American West and communed with nature. We were our own church. Marijuana became the sacrament we shared. By the time I reached Europe, I was a free-wheeling, free spirited, inquisitive young woman.

The Vatican is massive. Simply gargantuan. Incredibly more so than can be gleaned in photographs. Overwhelming in scale and artistic significance, it features design and artwork by artists of the highest renown, notably Michelangelo and Bernini. St. Pete's Square alone is huge, larger than two football fields and capable of holding 300,000 people. Giant statues of first century saints and popes gaze down from atop the colonnade. Walking inside the gigantic cathedral is sensory overload. Gold and gilt everywhere. Massive twisty columns. Incredible sculptures and paintings. Everywhere you turn more gorgeous marble, phenomenal granite, intricate tile. More artwork. More gold and gilt. Candles flickered in ornate alcoves. Sickly-sweet smelling incense wafted about. Gated stairs led down to eerie catacombs. People ambled from altar to altar, statue to statue, cameras clicking to capture the man-made majesty of the Papal Basilica of Saint Peter. It was hot and muggy, the crowds were pushy, and I was not impressed.

Instead of appreciating the valuable, glittering treasures inside, the cathedral produced a feeling of great vitriol in me. I felt total repulsion and horror at the smugness of the Catholic Church. Unbelievable riches spent in homage to "God" while man suffered, while the poor starved, while we killed peasants in Vietnam, while racism reigned, and while the *have-nots* sunk lower, and the *haves* rose on their backs. I couldn't even see the beauty of the great "Pieta" by Michelangelo. I was blinded by fury and disgust.

I sat under the golden canopy wondering why God allowed this. This was not my God. My God was about love, not riches. How could a religion based on the tenets of Jesus Christ, who preached love and taking care of the less fortunate, hold onto such treasures instead of using them to fund aid to those unsheltered, hungry, in need of medical assistance? I wanted an explanation. The vulgar riches of the Vatican offered little enticement to engage further with the Catholic Church.

In a defining moment, with full consciousness, I spit on the wall outside the enormous entry doors, turning my back on my childhood religion. It was important to me that I conduct a physical ritual of spiritual divorce. The Catholic Church had ruined God for me. If this was God, I wanted no part of Him. I would find another way to the Divine I knew existed. The Divine existed in the love I felt for my friends and the experiences I was undergoing. The Divine was everywhere, every day, not confined to a Mass, or the walls of a Church. I lived divinely by partaking in all the gifts of the universe. This was my God. I left that day, with a firmer sense than ever that there was another way to live in light and love, outside the pomp and circumstance of Catholicism.

I may have turned my back on God, but He never turned His back on me. That is the point of our life journey, isn't it? To find God, not religion. To develop our own relationship with the Divine. Religions are vehicles and tools to be used, not followed indiscriminately. As I was to find, there was much more God to come in my lifetime. But I had a much turbulent, roller-coaster, experiential living to do first.

28

Prodigal Daughter

As you have ascertained by now, my path to spiritual understanding was a rocky, wandering one. I went from spitting on the Vatican to exploring an array of spiritual practices, including astrology, Buddhism, Hinduism, Native American beliefs, and meditation. I suffered trauma and heartache but never lost my *joie de vivre*. I overdid everything, including sex, drugs, and Rock & Roll, which, frankly, became my religious substitute for years. Eventually, as I began to mature emotionally with therapy, I was able to recognize a more authentic self. Understanding myself better allowed me the opportunity to explore God more completely.

My spirituality started to coalesce in the later eighties but remained vague in practice.

Two momentous events in the mid-nineties caused me to have a "dark time of the soul," as Mother Theresa called it. The deaths of my beloved Mother, and then the death of my best friend JK had staggered me. JK had rebelled against traditional medical treatments for her breast cancer, choosing alternative practitioners. She still died. JK stayed with me for seventy-two straight hours when I couldn't be alone after being raped. She accompanied me to the hospital, to the police stations, to the line-ups. JK had talked me down from a bad acid trip when I lived in Boston, and she was in Cleveland. We were on the phone for four hours. I was at her wedding and the birth of her dear boys. She was the kind of bestie I could call and simply start talking without preamble. I was bereft I couldn't save her. Grief from these two losses laid me flat. And I was right back to my querulous question of God from twenty years earlier. Why?

I felt desperate and broken, with nowhere to turn. I couldn't sleep and was troubled by intrusive thoughts. I couldn't concentrate or think clearly. As a last resort, I asked God to help me. I was in that proverbial plane crash mode when you turn to faith as a last resort. As usual with God, He found me right where I was standing, befuddled and deeply depressed.

His grace appeared when a Catholic priest unexpectedly knocked on my front door in our Glen Park house in San Francisco. I hadn't even seen a priest in years. He was a new recruit to the blue-collar parish down the hill in the Sunnyside district. and was introducing himself to folks in the neighborhood. His appearance triggered a thought. Could the Church help me? I took hesitant steps back into worship, nervous but desperate.

The church building was familiar, with ornate carved marble and stained glass. There was the ancient communion rail, separating the altar from the people. Traditional small votive candles flickered in front of huge painted statues of saints. Although the inside was familiar, I found the Catholic Church massively changed from my youthful experiences. The priests were engaging, especially the younger ones. Full of love and welcoming. The Mass was a celebration, not drudgery. The diverse congregation seemed happy and engaged with the service. I was more than a little shocked and pleased.

Later, after moving from San Francisco to the neighboring city of San Mateo, I discovered my spiritual north, St. Bart's. The pastor, Father D, was a man of shorter stature but boundless energy, who described the gospels in terms of love. His velvety, sonorous, radio-ready voice infused our souls with fierce desire to act better. His mature preaching style captivated me. He made the gospels both intimate and universal. For the first time in my life, the Catholic Church started to make sense to me.

I now recognized church, no matter what denomination, as a community of like-minded souls who were also searching, trying, failing, getting up, falling, and trying again. I was surprised to find myself attending Mass more regularly, albeit anonymously. I started to glean the richer meanings of group prayer and worship. I even began to understand the components of Catholic Mass. First, we would listen to the Old Testament with its fiery, technicolor metaphors. Then we turned to the New Testament teachings of *how* to live. Jesus was the example to emulate. I became aware for the first time of the significance of the Eucharist. I was honored to participate in this 2000-year-old ritual of sharing bread and wine. The Eucharist wasn't for the holy. It was for people like me, the broken and the confused. I remember how shocked I was to find a visiting priest recount his years-long sojourn as a homeless alcoholic before finding Christ in the Eucharist. Who was I to stand on ceremony?

I was no longer concerned about the Church's riches. I was a long way from that naïve girl in St. Pete's Square all those years ago in Rome. I had seen the larger world up-close-and-personal in my Rock & Roll life. I knew grift, graft, and greed existed across the board. I also saw for the first time, however, how churches of all denominations carry the mantle of caring for the less fortunate in society. Parishes had food pantries, day-care, senior visitation, and other social services for the poor. It was eye-opening, especially when I accompanied a fellow parishioner into the homes of several poor families. He was giving out vouchers for new mattresses and clothing from the local thrift store. These small offerings made a dramatic difference to these quiet, unassuming families struggling to survive.

I met other men and women trying to live their faith, openly and honestly. We were a disparate group of singles, marrieds, fallen-aways, and strivers. We laughed, drank wine, and read the Bible. I didn't even own a bible when I started. Meanwhile my soul, starved for so long for real meaning, was like a sponge, absorbing all I was learning, and hungry for more. It was a heady time. I was truly the prodigal daughter being welcomed back with open arms. I had never understood this biblical story before. Now I was living it. I was floored to be accepted back into the fold with such love and acceptance.

Any concept of a faith community had been abstract, until I joined the community of St. Bart's. We were not only encouraged to actively participate in Church rituals but also expected to shoulder responsibility for the health and well-being of our faith community. That means partnership. This was difficult for me at times, largely because it made me confront my fears, especially the fear of *not being enough*. Standing up in front of the congregation reading a bible passage or saying hello to the stranger in the pew next to me, was strangely intimidating, despite being well versed in the public arena. In time however, I was drawn to becoming a Lector, reading sacred text during Mass. Then I became a Eucharistic Minister giving out the blessed bread and wine. Later I became an adult altar server assisting the priest during the Mass.

As I got more involved, Father reminded us- the Mass could not be celebrated alone. Jesus had said, "where two or more are gathered, do this in memory of me." I was amazed to see that community was defined as small as *you and me*. That challenged my sense of anonymity. While the Church of my youth was iconoclastic and emphasized our imperfectness, that imperfectness gave me an excuse to shrug off the demands of an engaged relationship with God. I kept God "up there" above me, not here, in the embrace of community.

I found spiritual fellowship isn't about knowing more or being better or being holier. It is understanding we are "enough" *right this minute*. This watershed understanding galvanizes us to right action with each other. It's not about having answers; it's about showing up wearing whatever spiritual clothes fit that day. We let others oversee situations because we doubt ourselves. Over time, I stepped forward, slowly gleaning how I could enjoy active adult participation in my faith community at St. Bart's. It was a powerful lesson of grace, humility, to remaining open to following the Spirit, no matter where it leads.

29

Mystical Journey

Our search to understand our existence follows a well-trod path. Whether we find spiritual solace in God, a Higher Power, Buddha, Yahweh, Brahma, a forest, the night sky, the nothingness of being, or the smile of a grandchild, I honestly believe we all long for meaning and connection. This chimerical story of my own stuttering pursuit remains the most significant chapter of my faith journey.

While attending St. Bart's satisfied some of my needs, my yearnings for a more personally substantive relationship with God remained. Friends on the spiritual path urged me to commit to the Spiritual Exercises of St. Ignatius at Mercy Center, a local retreat house. St. Ignatius of Loyola wrote the Spiritual Exercises as a simple set of meditations, prayers, and various other mental exercises, generally conducted over a period of thirty days. My particular retreat program ran for thirty Monday nights—nine months—of engaged contemplation, journaling, group discussion and prayer.

My spiritual life at the time was dry. I was restless. Fr. D, who had captivated me with his enthralling sermons, had to leave the parish. My hospice work was full-time and fulfilling, but I had an extremely toxic executive director. Secretly, I *still* desperately wanted to stop drinking. I continued to suffer from overconsumption of alcohol. I was at the end of my rope with my inability to stop, with the blackouts, the debilitating hangovers, the daily drinking. I had beat a daily addiction to cocaine in the '80s, but I couldn't get a handle on the drinking. I didn't tell a soul about my secret wish to give up alcohol. Not even Honey. Hell, I could barely admit this to myself in my heart of hearts. I threw myself into the Spiritual Exercises of St. Ignatius as a last resort.

St. Ignatius suggests you insert yourself directly into the gospel story to fully understand Jesus. Take any story of Jesus preaching and *embed* yourself into the action. Perhaps you are in the crowd trying to get a better view of Jesus, so you push your way to the front. You feel claustrophobic being mashed into the surging throng. The jostling crowd feels threatening. The aggressiveness of the apostles protecting Jesus intimidates you. You have trouble breathing with all the dust. It is hot and sweaty. You are dying of thirst but didn't bring your wine-skin. You are there with Jesus, inside looking out, not outside looking in.

This was completely foreign to me. Like many of us, when I prayed, God was an entity outside of me, above me—over there somewhere—higher. Yet, I did as instructed. Our very first reading of the exercises centered on John the Baptist and Jesus, from the gospel of John 1:35-39. It's about two disciples following Jesus. Truthfully, I didn't know if I could insert myself into this scene. But I settled down and started to pray.

Suddenly I was on the bank of a sluggish river, under a wizened tree. John the Baptist was standing erect in knee-high water, enjoying the beautiful day. The sky was a crystalline blue with a tepid breeze, and muddy water swirled lazily against his legs. It was desert hot. I sat in meager shade on the stream bank, drowsy in the heat.

I had come to this spot because I had heard that John the Baptist knew where the Savior was. I didn't know what a *Savior* was, but I was alert to the *next big thing*. That's how I thought of Jesus. It was not unlike how I had scouted hundreds of bands during my rock years, always alert to the *next big thing*.

As I sat there, I heard John the Baptist, say pointedly but casually, "There he is, the Lamb of God." John then gave me a penetrating, sidelong look. I immediately gleaned his underlying meaning. I turned and saw Jesus receding down a well-trod path away from me. I scrambled up and ran after him, like one might run after a favorite celebrity they spot walking down the street. I was a little breathless in my haste. Then Jesus unexpectedly halted, turned around and looked at me. I stumbled on a rock, pulling up abruptly.

"What do you want?" He asked. I was embarrassed to be caught chasing after him like a silly fan, then tripping over my own feet. I bent down and pretended to adjust my sandal while I tried to think of something clever to say to Him. To hide my discomfiture, I asked him where he was staying.

"Why don't you come with me and see," He replied. So, I did. We walked a short way down a hard-packed, rocky path to His cliffside house. It was a one room adobe hut with a large stone hearth. A crude bench sat before the hearth. The kitchen table was of solid, rough hewn wood with two crudely carved chairs. There was a large window over an earthen sink. You could see for what seemed like miles out that window. Sky, clouds, mountains, prairies, desert, rivers. Seeing the expansiveness of the world through that window was ineffable. I felt like all of eternity was on view. Jesus offered me a chair to sit down, and I did.

This is how I ended up in Jesus' kitchen, where a whole new chapter of my journey was revealed to me in prayer as the retreat months progressed. I revisited this kitchen on many occasions to talk with Jesus and gaze out that window. Other times we would sit on the bench gazing into the fire, while evil growled and roared directly behind our backs. All those demonic miscreants and emotional wounds were back there. Fears of being attacked, nightmares, insecurities and hurt were bundled up in devilish type beings, more animal than man, were wrestling for my soul, snarling and thrashing. The sound of their gnashing teeth was terrifying. Although I wanted to run away, I knew I was safe, sitting there with Jesus, calmly discussing important matters. We never turned around to look at the evil miasma behind us. We simply sat together time after time, until every one of my scary monsters gave up and dissipated into nothingness.

As the months of retreat rolled on, my talks with Jesus expanded to include the Father and the Holy Spirit. In Catholicism, the Father, Son, and Holy Spirit make up the Holy Trinity, which is one God in three Divine persons. I found new understanding in the Trinity, which became a metaphysical touchstone for me. God is both Father *and* Mother yet *genderless*, overseeing eternity with an embrace that encompassed all existence. Jesus walks with us, our brother, as perfect role model. The Holy Spirit guides us through thick and thin with protective instincts—if we listen (the challenge of free will). The enormity of God is too much for our human understanding. Describing Him with multiple personas makes sense to me.

I often visited the Trinity on a familiar mountaintop. The Father is sitting on what I imagined was a very solid chair, not unlike the rough furniture I saw in Jesus' house. I am sitting on the Father's knee, one arm on His shoulder and another around Jesus, who is standing beside us. The Holy Spirit, a white dove as envisioned in centuries of old master paintings, is perched on my shoulder. The moment is always sublime. These spiritual avatars remain very real to me.

I embraced the process of the Exercises at Mercy Center with my entire being. A few short weeks after starting the program, I quit drinking. For good. I asked God for help from the most hidden recesses of my soul, and He answered. It was a tremendous relief to be out from under the yoke of that genetic addiction. I haven't had a drink since October 23, 2006. A few months after that I realized it was time to make other changes. I knew without a doubt a new path was beckoning. Those mystical, magical exercises had captured my soul.

30

Unexpected Faith

After delving more deeply into faith through the Spiritual Exercises of St. Ignatius, my husband and I decided to move to Phoenix, Az. to be with my family. It seemed like a perfect opportunity for me to rediscover my multi-generational family as an adult. What I did not expect to find was a spiritual chapter as meaningful as any that had come before. Leaving San Mateo meant leaving my tight-knit church community of mentors— and my retreat center. Leaving them left me spiritually bereft.

Lo and behold, after arriving in Phoenix, my great-nephews told me about their new parish priest. Fr. G had long hair like Jesus and rode his bike everywhere. He also liked the Grateful Dead and used the Grateful Dead's "dancing bear and rose" image to sign off his weekly letters in the church bulletin. I had left spiritual nirvana of northern California only to discover a Grateful Dead loving, Jesus emulating priest? Holy Cow. I found the parish to be as welcoming as a Grateful Dead concert too. What a unique and effective example of God's grace in action.

I inched my way into the parish by helping with the annual parish festival. Before long I was knee deep in the hoopla of this parish on the edge of the desert. I was gobsmacked by the down-to-earth folks I found practicing their faith. Our church was a plain re-purposed gym, but a more sacred space you would never find. Fr. G was inspiring, environmentally conscious, and he never stood on ceremony. Usually dressed in jeans and a tee, the only times he wore his clerical collar was Easter and Christmas, (so those who only attended on those high holy days would know he was the real Pastor). He was of the people and by the people. His commitment to the tenets of Jesus' love inspired the most hardened, conservative, Arizona heart. Fr. G came over to our house occasionally, to relax and listen to the Grateful Dead. Honey would cook him a vegan meal and he would be able to relax with nice hot meal. Since Fr. G lived rather ascetically, surviving on the simplest of fares, we were always happy to feed him.

After a few years, Fr. G was transferred to another parish. Fr. B, a native of Uganda and a proud MBA graduate of Notre Dame, took his place. He was the opposite of Fr. G in style but not in faith and love. Fr. B loved everyone and had a broad smile that wouldn't quit. He and I were a mutual admiration society. Fr. B challenged me to develop and share my spiritual talents. I found myself on the altar more often than off. I lectored at mass, distributed the holy Eucharist, read the prayers of the faithful, wrote gospel reflections, fed the poor, educated on hospice/dementia/palliative care, led prayer groups, and took on parish leadership roles.

One favorite memory of Fr. B came from a parish festival. That day Notre Dame was playing and important game, so a large-screen digital television was set up outside, near the bar. A crowd of twenty to thirty settled to watch, Fr. B taking a seat in front. Everything went smoothly until kick-off when the screen went black. Horror of horrors! There arose an outcry. Fr. B, always one to seize the moment, reached deep into his pocket for his prayer rosary. He stood and held his rosary dramatically aloft, as if asking God for a miracle. *Exactly* at that moment, the screen came to life again. A miracle! Fr. B bowed to the deafening cheers.

When I left to return to northern California nine years later, members of my prayer group gave me a warm-hearted going-away party. Fr. B wrote a heartfelt letter of thanks to me in the bulletin. I was sad to leave those good people. Expecting nothing when I arrived, I left with an abundance of grace. St. Bens turned out to be a surprising chapter in the book of my spiritual awareness. Those people lived their faith so completely.

I continue to carry the gifts I received from those years close to my heart. They are a constant and welcome reminder of what we find when we're not looking and just let God be God.

31

Free Falling

I had a contented twenty years of faith in the Catholic Church before I lost my loyalty. I mean, completely lost it. Not with God, or Jesus, or the Holy Spirit. Not with the Divine, the All-Knowing, The One "Whose Name We Cannot Say." My mistake was reading the Pennsylvania Grand Jury Report on Priest Abuse. I lost it with the Catholic Church and their abysmal, horrific, and injurious response to victims who had been sexually abused by priests. This information sent me into a tumbling spiritual free fall.

I'm not sure what drew me to that Grand Jury report. We all knew about abusive priests. There was one at our upscale parish when I was growing up. I knew some of the families involved. The details did not come out until thirty years late. No one spoke about these incidents. Through the years, despite evidence to the contrary, most everyone denied how widespread the ghastly abuse was in their communities. No matter what parish, there were whispered stories about past clergy who had left under clouds of suspicion or mysterious circumstances.

By that mild summer day in 2018, when the world crashed in around me, I was ensconced back in Northern California. The campus of my delightful retirement village had a glass jewel-box of a church, set in a stand of gorgeous California oaks. The attendees were the old and the incredibly old. I joked that I was the youngest person at service, as I was only in my mid-sixties.

Outside of its lovely natural setting, this parish did little to meet my spiritual needs. The priests were jovial and easy-going. Knowing their flock were closer to eternal life than not, they kept things light and status quo. The preaching consisted of jokes and tame interpretations of the gospels. We showed up and that was enough. These priests weren't going to ask much more of us.

I looked around half-heartedly for a better intellectual fit. But the convenience factor— being two minutes away—won out. Instead of finding a new worship home, I stayed where I was and joined their Monday morning meditation group. This small, dedicated assemblage provided the inspiration I needed. We gathered on folding chairs in the room also used for AA meetings and to store seasonal decorations, stacks of outdated hymnal books and found items. Breathing quietly and meditating on a brief reading was followed by a gentle discussion. Those were quiet, contemplative mornings in the shady church glen overlooking the polo field. They filled my needs temporarily. I also moved from attending church to volunteering with the homeless. I became the Wednesday receptionist at a family shelter for homeless families. I advocated for better solutions for our unsheltered neighbors in my town. It was a time of growing awareness. Life motored along nicely.

But there I was, bored on a mild summer's day in 2018, when I decided to pull up the Pennsylvania Grand Jury Report on Priest Abuse. Our priests had acknowledged the report but said the Church had taken steps to make sure these "things" never happened again. But had they? I became more horrified the more I read. I became distraught. My stomach turned. I couldn't even finish that report. I wanted to finish reading, as a way of honoring those victims and their stories. But I couldn't. I just couldn't.

Story after story of children and their parents complaining, of church hierarchy ignoring these complaints, or threatening parishioners who spoke up. Page after page of how the victims were abused at such tender ages, children left to the evils of sexual abuse. The extent and complicity of the abuses were breathtaking/heartbreaking, while the perpetrators quietly transferred from one parish to another, where new victims awaited.

My heart shattered—perhaps because of my own powerless feeling when I was sexually traumatized. I had not forgotten how helpless I felt after being assaulted when I was twenty years old. I couldn't imagine being a teen or pre-teen. Like these young people, I felt betrayed. I had trusted the Catholic Church with my soul. At that moment, the Catholic Church became dead to me.

I spent months angry and bereft. Bereft because I had lost my community, my rituals, my hymns, my people. Angry because the Catholic Church acted with such deliberate cruelty and unChrist like evil. *Was I so blind and accepting?* Now, for the second time in my life, years after my spitting at the Vatican, I was done with Catholicism. Not Christ. But the Catholic church.

For quite some time I felt unsettled, estranged, sad. I could not find my way back to a pattern of worship or engagement with a community. I felt the spiritual rug had been yanked out from under me. Which way to turn? How to salvage my faith? What did faith mean to me? Did I even have faith? In retrospect, reading the Grand Jury report on abusive priests was a necessary step for me. Perhaps I had become complacent and needed a reminder that the church is me. I represent Jesus. God isn't out there. God is in me. Priests, bishops, popes, they are just men—broken, imperfect men. I have the power to reflect the Divine, celebrate the Divine, and engage the Divine.

I realized I'd been walking toward this more authentic interpretation of the Divine all along, this place where community is important but organized religion not as important. It's no secret that I never agreed with the tenets of the Catholic Church. Their man-made rules on divorce, abortion, homosexuality, women priests, and married priests all felt like burrs under my saddle. I was able to immerse myself in the church because so many of my fellow Catholics felt the same way as. We just never voiced it aloud. Our disagreements with the Church were tacitly understood. Now I wondered—was it time to start living my faith more authentically?

Possibly I needed the grand jury report to awaken me to the broader, wider possibilities of a more meaningful existence. Maybe I needed that anguish in my soul to push myself in terms of growing up spiritually and accepting self-responsibility. Perhaps it was time for me to climb back onto that dusty, rocky path where I found Jesus all those years ago. He showed me then that everything that breathes has a soul. Maybe it was time for me to devote my worship to saving the earth, a living entity. Or feeding and clothing the poor, my living neighbors. Or protecting animals, all of which have living souls.

Instead of worshiping Jesus, why couldn't I just try to live like Him? Be kind. Be loving. Help others. Give my time and talents to those less fortunate. Fulfill social and moral obligations as a productive member of society. Placing these tenets in the forefront of my activities has helped me feel engaged with God more fully.

Being in the secular world, however, is rougher, tougher, and crasser than when bolstered by like-minded souls. Also,

I'm prone to laziness and appreciate the inspiration I get from seeing others practice their faith. I like worshiping in community. It's bonding, engaging and inspiring both physically and spiritually. Without it I find myself adrift and spiritually lonely, my prayer life and meditation haphazard at best.

Occasionally I will find inspiration on the Internet. While attending a dear friend's mother's ninety-eighth birthday, I was introduced to an engaging young pastor in a distant church. Rev. TJ is a third-generation preacher with an exhilarating knowledge of faith. This church, two hours from my home, has a diverse, urban community. I began listening to Reverend's gospel reflections online, during the pandemic. His illuminating preaching continually enlightened me to deeper understanding about what is asked of me in faith. I was enthralled by his ability to connect current-day challenges to events that happened eons ago. This holy man reignited my passion for community and for Christ for a while.

But alas, I find myself still struggling to reconcile religion intellectually. I despair that the Evangelicals have ruined Christianity for the rest of us. Sometimes I question whether I can follow Christianity at all, seeing the great harm religion has caused throughout human history. Still, I search for a local group to fill my spiritual needs. I know I thrive on the discipline of ritual and service. I miss acknowledging a greater power in a public setting. But for the time being, I muck about doing the best I can, yet another chapter in my continuum of faith.

The only thing I know to be really true is God. God lives in me. Each breath is the constant reminder of that. My faith remains embedded in my existence. God exists increasingly in moments of everyday living. Nature abounds with His creativity and majesty in trees, birds, sky, sunsets. Each morning I wake up with gratitude and thanksgiving.

Every day I ask for guidance from the Holy Spirit and the openness to hear it. Daily I ask Jesus to guide me, love me, forgive me.

I feel God all the time. In late-night laughter with my husband. In the rosebush outside my window. While stroking the cats. When driving to the store past expansive vineyards teeming with red grapes. In thick white clouds. Rain. In enough milk for my coffee. When I realize how amazingly our bodies are designed—I thank God—for giving me this extraordinary gift of life.

Lastly, know this. Whether it's people I love, natural beauty I cherish in my midst, or a well-reasoned thought that makes it to my page, I always give thanks. THANK YOU, GOD. THANK YOU. THANK YOU. And maybe, just maybe, that's enough to get your heavenly conversation started.

PART SEVEN

Epilogues

32

Reflections on #MeToo

I didn't write about my rape experience to garner sympathy. It's not necessarily cathartic either. I'm *compelled* to write, so that *you* would know what your Mom, sister, wife, or girlfriend has endured. It may surprise you to know that *one in six women have been victimized by sexual assault.* If six Moms drive in your school carpool, one of those six Moms has been sexually violated. If you have six female relatives, one of them has been sexually forced. Of the six women you know at work, one of them has been assaulted. These facts are from RAINN (Rape, Abuse & Incest National Network). Most victims are between the ages of twelve and thirty-four years of age (I was twenty and a junior in college.) Fifty-five percent of rapes occur at or near the victim's home (I was yards from my dorm).

Hewing to this last fact, at the time of my rape, in the fall of 1971, there were two other instances of sexual assault within a six-block radius of our dorm. Two friends walking to their campus apartment were accosted on a street corner at knife point and both were raped. A rapist broke into an apartment where three other friends were terrorized for hours. These are just the ones I was told about. Most of my friends were leery of sharing such dispiriting news with me.

The #MeToo movement has put society on notice about what is no longer acceptable sexual behavior between persons. At the time I was in the music business, however, being a woman working in a male dominated field meant going along to get along. You saw and did things that were routine—if unmentionable. I've read scores of comments on social media asking how the women working for these men could enable their injurious behavior. The reality is most women didn't have a choice if they wanted to keep their jobs. If someone asked me to cover for them when they were fooling around, I covered for them. And we didn't lose any sleep over it.

My own experiences with male chauvinism were routine. Traveling in Europe, I was once introduced to a minor royal who worked for a record company. Shortly after I was introduced to him in a heavily decorated, gilded hotel suite, he whipped out his penis expecting servicing. A male colleague in attendance hurriedly stopped him, explaining I was "management." Another man I worked with would casually fondle his genitals while chatting business with me in his office. An industry giant would rub my back proprietarily and continually, even in business meetings with associates. Eventually I got up the nerve to tell him to knock it off. He was sullen and petulant afterward. Crowded into a taxi on the way to a rock club, the man next to me laid his head on my breasts, while extolling the virtues of my pillow like boobs. These are just a few examples of how common place it was for men to overstep boundaries, back in the day. None of this bothered me. It was harmless, really. Boys play. It wasn't dangerous. It didn't involve guns or nakedness in freezing weather or kidnapping. That was just sex. Nothing at all. Just sex.

In reflection though, I am horrified at what I—women— put up with in our careers. I'm ashamed I didn't stand up when I saw women being taken advantage of, even if they didn't realize it themselves. The #MeToo movement hasn't just been a cultural tsunami but also a healing salvo for those of us who suffered silently while feeling powerless.

I made choices all along to live my life like a man. Perhaps I was being protective of myself. I did what I wanted when I wanted, with whom I wanted and wherever I wanted. I was not a soft girly girl. I could drink more prodigiously, ingest more drugs, and stay awake longer than anyone, without a crack in my façade. I never lost control, which is revealing. Obviously, I felt the best way to protect myself was by never ceding control. I also had no spiritual compass, which led me to poor behavior and personal betrayals that I regret.

The fast-changing cultural mores and the empowerment of feminists certainly influenced my sexual coming of age. In hindsight though, at least some of my promiscuous behavior reveals how deeply I smothered my fears and simply took what came along. Possibly I was trying to control the narrative to keep myself safe. I was well into adulthood before I grew into some semblance of a more emotionally mature woman.

Writing about being raped in college is a giant leap for me. I remain irrationally terrified of admitting to this dark moment. No one wants to confess to being kidnapped at gunpoint and taken into an alley and raped. After a lifetime, perhaps I can safely unwrap that tightly wound bundle of nerves I've carried for so long. Maybe I can step into that abyss of vulnerability and not fall apart. All these years later. It's been a long lesson. One I'm not convinced will ever be completely over.

Yes, it's only now, in my late sixties, that I realize maybe I can feel safe. But not because I overcame my fears. Not because I was determined to not let it stop me from living my dreams. Sadly, it's because I'm a senior. I'm lumpy, and dumpy, and gray. No longer attractive prey. Not prey. At last, not prey. A dismal statement, at best.

I admit to not always understanding what is considered sexual assault today. An unwanted kiss or unwarranted hug seems innocuous, not traumatic. But then I remember it's about power not sex. If you are troubled from sexual trauma, simply know you are not alone. For those of you lucky enough to escape sexual assault, remember this: It did happen. It does happen. It will happen. (RAINN.org)

33

Golden Grads

I had the honor of speaking at my Fiftieth High School reunion in 2019. Four generations of women in my family, and my husband's family, have been educated at that private, all-girls Catholic school. Sitting in that gorgeous, restored mansion, I delivered an unexpected reflection of the times we lived through and a rumination on trusting the Spirit. As I pointed out to the three hundred attendees, the class of 1969 was a bit different than the classes that came before us. We were knee-deep in the generational changes sweeping across America. Our student years saw us taking baby steps along with the rest of America toward equality and justice. We sang Woody Guthrie, Peter, Paul and Mary, and American spirituals at our hootenannies. We created Students with a Purpose (SWAP), a cultural exchange with black students from cross town. We explored new social opportunities and pushed the boundaries. We lived through the assassinations of Martin Luther King and Bobby Kennedy. We studied why "No Man is an Island" and read Kierkegaard in religion class, unafraid to develop adult sensibilities with God, thanks to our brilliant teachers who respected our minds, our hearts, and our souls.

Our adult lives have reflected these generational cultural shifts in American life. We were college freshmen when the first Earth Day was celebrated on April 22, 1970. Kent State closely followed and that was just the beginning. We are the first generation of working mothers. We are the first generation of openly blended families. Our class of 1969 accomplished professional achievements, community achievements, and spiritual achievements unimaginable fifty years earlier.

I recounted for my contemporaries how the Spirit always guided me, even when following that guidance made no discernible sense. I described how I knew I was destined for San Francisco; confident I would go there and meet my heroes. I told them how I met my husband by the Spirit literally tapping me on the shoulder, saying to me, go back and talk to that man. Then, when I wanted to leave Rock & Roll for a more meaningful life of service, the Spirit guided me to Hospice. I reminded them that this same Spirit has made us what we are today: ground breakers, leaders, mothers, grandmothers, aunts, colleagues, friends.

I pointed out the importance of reflecting this reality to our grandchildren, children, families, our communities, and the world at large. This absolute knowledge and trust in the Spirit, our feelings of empowerment, and these feelings of being enough. We live in an age of change and depersonalization, a period of haves and have-nots, an age where human to human contact is being curtailed by health concerns. It is more necessary than ever to let our gifts shine brightly, so everyone can feel and respond to the Spirit, everyone can feel empowered, and everyone can feel that they, too, can contribute. This is the human value. We all count.

A hearty applause followed my speech. Graduate after golden grad stopped me on my way out of the event to thank me for what I said. Old ladies barely able to walk lauded me. Many expressed their admiration. Many felt inspired. The principal pulled me aside and wondered if I would consider returning

and speaking to the student body as a whole. Attendees continued to reach out and text me for days. Naturally, I was happy
and humbled by their response. I left feeling empowered and
enthused. I had put speaking and writing on the back burner
for a time. This was obvious proof that I was meant to revisit
these gifts and re-evaluate their place in my life. I was buzzing
in the aftermath of praise and attention.

That evening there was a cocktail party for our class of
golden graduates. I had taken a special dress to wear to that
event. But when I started to dress, feelings of insecurity arose.
My self-confidence vanished into thin air, replaced by a feeling
of unworthiness. I fretted about the dress I had chosen. How
could I possibly wear it and show my fat arms? My only bra was
all wrong. My clothes were not right. My entire talk was a lie. I
was old, fat, ugly. I went to the cocktail party in the same outfit
I had worn at the luncheon. My speaking attire. I was embarrassed for myself. Who wears the same clothes at two different
events? How quickly I had gone from the heights of empowerment to the depths of self-doubt. A perfect example of bad
self-talk.

I must laugh, I'm so flawed. Life is steadily three steps
forward and two steps back. See, I'm just like you—constantly
beating myself up for being human and having doubts, fears,
imperfections. I'm the same tangled human mess, striving for
better. Isn't this the perfect metaphor for our lives? Lessons
learned, repeatedly, until they stick. Again, and again.

Luckily, I overcame my doubts about the reunion in the
illuminating light of next day. That's what I've learned about
these feelings of not being enough. Bring those feelings of anxiety into the bright sunshine of truth and knowledge. Don't let
them fester. Don't stop being an example. You may fall into the
same hole multiple times until you learn to finally walk around

it. That's the beauty of life. You always have another chance to follow your muse, make things right, do the right thing.

Thank goodness the reaction of my contemporaries and those in attendance at the reunion galvanized me. It was time for me to stop feeling like an impostor and trust my gifts. I marshaled my emotional forces and started outlining this book in my head. By the time I returned home to California, I had scribbled out a rough three-page outline. It's never too late to trust the Spirit. Repeat after me. Never. Too. Late.

34

Tribute to Our Rock & Roll Youth

Why is it when you watch a memorial celebration slide show, it's your own life that flashes before your eyes? That's what happened when I attended a memorial for Freddie Herrera, a recently deceased nightclub owner who was a kingpin in the Bay Area during the 1970s and 1980s. Heck, I was still wet-behind-the-ears in 1975, when my blues-rock boyfriend Nick Gravenites introduced me to this man. While I did not know this gentleman well, I sure knew his music clubs. Besides featuring the best local and national talent around, his clubs in Berkeley, Palo Alto and in San Francisco were a locus for us Bay Area music scenesters.

The memorial was organized by my old music biz pal Jim Burgin and musician/emcee Dave Martin. It became a homage to my earliest days in San Francisco, when music was still fun, and not a business. It was an evening of appreciation for those early years, by honoring Freddie, who had been one of us, before we became professionals and made careers out of our passion for music. The musical tribute onstage featured popular local bands from those halcyon days who regularly played those funky nightclubs.

The upscale nightspot hosting the memorial was packed to overflowing. People hung off the balcony and crammed into tiny two-top cocktail tables. While still plush looking at night, the venue's torn carpeting and scuffed floors looked a bit shopworn during the early daylight portion of the event. Not too different from those of us attending. Old friends who had sported long-hair were now bald. Grey hair was the norm, not the exception. People forewent shots of alcohol, opting for bottles of water. Oldsters sat comparing body aches and surgeries in side-chatter. Colleagues who had snubbed me years earlier, greeted me like a long-lost bestie. The heady scene highlighted the resilient connections we made back in those salad days.

In the 70s and 80s, the Bay Area music scene was as vibrant as its older sibling, the psychedelic '60s, though it garnered less attention. These were the bygone glory days when regional bands could make a living playing clubs in the seven counties that make up the Bay Area. And future superstars—Petty, the Ramones, Prince—could use these clubs to expand their national fan base. Who can forget Prince on his Dirty tour, laying claim to his brilliant future? The Jerry Garcia Band played so often they were considered the house band.

At the memorial, musicians who had played those clubs regularly, gathered to pay homage and recreate their past hits. In a lovely moment of synchronicity, my old flame/mentor Nick Gravenites gave a rousing tribute speech harkening back to the earliest days of the scene. Nick and Michael Bloomfield had helped Freddie start his first Keystone night club in SF. After a nostalgic slide show, the evening's music began.

Emcee David Martin of the Lloyds, had put together a fantastic house band of players from back in the day. I watched amazed as Tommy Dunbar, the guitar player from The Rubinoos, skid absolutely unironically on his knees across the stage in time honored tradition, furiously riffing on his guitar. I listened as the lead singer of the band Earthquake, Johnny O'Dea, roared through "Friday On My Mind" in a voice honed in hundreds of raucous clubs. When Martin brought up the great Annie Sampson of Stoneground fame, she showed us great voices don't die but instead become impossibly better. Greg Kihn, a local fave with one giant hit song ("Jeopardy") made us all feel a sense of nostalgia by introducing his son on guitar. These were flashbacks to the '70s when our lives were still open-ended—our futures murky in want, need, and Rock & Roll.

Truth be told, most often I don't attend these events. But when guitar virtuosos Roy Rogers and Johnny "V" Vernazza got up for an old-fashioned guitar-slinger showdown, the room became electric. Again, that indescribable rush of hearing music played live washed over me, along with a warm river of memories. Live music had been my North Star for most of my music career, so feeling the familiar adrenaline surge in the intimate context of friends and family was wildly satisfying. When blues star, Elvin Bishop, mostly retired, got up to end the show, we yelled out lustily. By the time he got to his encore of "Dancing Shoes, I have to say, this old, jaded rocker girl got up and danced, creaky knees and all. It felt good to enjoy the music with my buddies, just like in the good old days. We did good. Rock lives on. And so do we.

Once you've been through the fires of Rock & Roll, regardless of whether you were an artist, manager, promoter, publicist, radio geek, record store, record label, or critic, you're brothers and sisters in the club forever. I have never laughed harder than with my music biz pals. It's been such a wondrous life, with so many good people. I made a lifetime of friends and marvelous memories. I am deeply grateful for my lengthy career in the music business. I did what I set out to do. I worked with some of the best musical artists of my generation. I made my own tiny mark on San Francisco music history. And I lived to tell the tale.

35

Wisdom Keepers

Now that many of us are going into the third chapter of our lives, it is so important to remember we are the Wisdom Keepers. Our accumulated knowledge is vital and should be passed on to subsequent generations. Not because we have been right. We've been wrong way more than right. Climate change alone shows us how greatly we have failed in certain arenas. It's important to share our experiences because of our *accrued emotional intelligence*. We have braved the storms and marched onward. It's this resilience that is important for us to model. It's about knowing *we all count*, no matter how things turn out, as long as we continue to move forward.

I feel in these times of tiny screens, masks, and social distancing, it is more important than ever to reconnect with the Spirit and acknowledge its beneficence on our behalf. I am convinced the more we disconnect from human life, and discount the power of the Soul, ignoring the Spirit, the more the human species with will be reduced to one-dimensional, soulless living. I daresay our very Souls, as well as our species, are at stake—especially now that we see the rippling effects of a worldwide pandemic. Isolation is bad for all of us on the planet.

Do not let technology fool you into thinking it replaces human interaction. Our souls depend on our humanity to thrive, not technology. When our worlds are defined by devices it is easy to limit our view of the world to what's working for us. The problem is that when you enter that *information funnel* you see only your world, not our world, the world we all live in together. Having a living soul demands we engage in community, diversity, and storytelling, honoring divergent paths. Even if it's as simple as saying hello to a stranger on the street. It's essential we mirror respect to others. We are all responsible for the world we live in. You can't use an app to show compassion or comfort someone for real.

All my past seems like yesterday. The world I knew as a child is gone. The world I knew in my twenties is gone. The world I knew in my thirties is gone. And onward. The only world that exists is today. And today decides tomorrow. Our futures are ours to make. I went from a hard living, highly visible Rock & Roll insider to an anonymous hospice worker ministering to the needs of the seriously ill. Who could have imagined? Certainly not me. But it is this exact trajectory, along with my continuing spiritual quest, that shaped me into who I am today.

Looking back with the vantage of time, I have accomplishments I'm proud of in my life. But I was a failure many more times than not. Many more times! Ironically, neither achievements nor missteps seem important as my life waxes and wanes in the breadth of these older years. At this chapter in my life, I do not believe what we accomplish in life to be our purpose for living. I reason it's about constantly challenging ourselves to become better human beings. Listening. Hearing. Seeing. Practicing kindness. Service. Unconditional love. Actions, not words. Kindness is my motto. If we can be kind to our fellow souls, I believe we will be successful in this world, regardless of other achievements or failures.

I had no understanding of Spirit when I began my adult life. Coming from a buttoned-up society, I was not in touch with my body or my soul or how they might be interconnected. It's taken me a lifetime of dubious effort, then intentional striving, to hone my internal powers of listening to this unseen, inexplicable entity. I have shunned it, blamed it, refused it, and hidden it. I've cursed myself, cried out, begged, and railed against it. Yet, Spirit has remained ever ready with its prompts and nudging. It's impossible to alienate.

Spirit is universal to all of us. There is no religion attached to this presence. No worries about heaven, hell, guilt, bargaining, although I too have those residual elements of early childhood indoctrination lurking in me. No dependence on meditating or chanting or praying, although these can be valuable, important tools. It's not reliant on any special concept of God or any other deities. It's dependent only on the concept of the Soul. Every living being has a Soul. Every Soul has a Spirit. Spirit is always working on behalf of the Soul.

Let me end with a recent experience that capsulizes my beliefs.

My brother Rick died while I was fine-tuning this book. Since we were especially close as the two babies, his death, while not a surprise, devastated me emotionally. I turned to grief counseling over zoom during the pandemic, which was immensely helpful. I also prayed and meditated as best I could. Snippets really, of fractured prayers and unrealized meditations.

One day I found myself especially hard hit by a wave of grief. I fervently began to meditate, asking God for help. I felt like I was drowning. As I sat with my eyes closed, my breathing steady, a clear image appeared in my consciousness. I was walking through a field of deep, flaming pits. A narrow, crumbling path curved through these smoking, earthy cauldrons. I was afraid to step forward, paralyzed in my fear. Suddenly my old pal Jesus appeared beside me. He bent down and slapped the ground, to show me the path was solid. Then he actually took both hands and widened the path for me (somewhat like how you are able to widen an image on your screen).

Still, I remained too fearful to move. Jesus then put-up waist-high iron guardrails, which ran the length of the curving path to ensure my safety. As gaseous steam belched out of these minefields of fire and molten lava, I saw I now had a clear, safe path through the mayhem in front of me. The image then dissipated, I came back to earth and was left to ponder what it all meant. I could almost swear I felt the heat of those gaseous pits still on my arms. It was that real.

Weeks of grieving went by. Finally, my brother was buried, after months of COVID delay. I was meditating when another image came to me unbidden. Now, I was standing on the other of the viper pit of flames. I had been journaling, talking to my counselor, and sitting with my grief instead of running from it. Although I suffered with grief, I did not let it cower me. I embraced all of it, the good, the bad and the ugly. These earthly efforts insured I would reach the other side, metaphorically. Jesus was there standing with me; proud I had safely walked through the danger zone.

Yet I was still transfixed looking back at what I had walked through. It felt dangerously fascinating to me. I could not tear my eyes away from the destructive fiery area I had safely navigated. I was in danger of remaining stuck at the scene of my emotional turmoil. Jesus gently but firmly turned my head away from that which was now behind me and made me look forward. The view, as always when I was with Him, was limitless and expansive. An amazing scene stretched out before me of hills, trees, mountains, streams, sky, world. I had made it through to the other side. It was time for new beginnings, not looking back. I stepped away from the mayhem and strode forward.

And that is what God is to me.

No matter where you find your own version of God or how you define the Spirit, I wrote this book to inspire you. It is my humble hope these stories encourage you to step through your own fears. My life is your life. The details may be different, but human challenges are universal. My intention was to write as honestly as possible, so you know it is never too late to change, never too late to embrace new passions, never too late to redefine your own journey.

May your soul rock with boldness. May you trust the Spirit. May you always be blessed. Amen and Namaste.

Acknowledgments

Thank you for reading my book. I'm humbled and appreciative.

Please note, these are my personal reflections and my perceptions of events. Others may have their own perspectives. I'd like to thank my remaining sisters, Michele Condon (Mikki) and Judith Dostal. Everyone knows sister #3, Mikki, is my "other M", while Judy and I certainly have had our share of adventures too. Special shout outs to all the Parsons, Condon, Wrabetz, Bee, Donaldson, Wade, Dostal, Fell and Bates extended families.

I'd like to thank my remarkable editor Ida Rae Egli who helped me craft this book, and encouraged me every step of the way. Thanks to my publisher Waights Taylor Jr. (a southern brother) and the McCaa Books family.

Big thanks to friends who read the book in various pre-publication forms: Hiya Swanhuyser especially, Mary Armstrong, Jacky Sarti, Jonah Raskin, Debby Dill, Bill Wannamaker, Marsha Armstrong. Additionally, I am grateful for Marcus Taylor, Billy Douglas, T Murdock, Noreen Copeland, and Susan Duryea, Sue Finn, and the Hollywood Book Festival. Special thanks to Dr. Rachel Remen, healer.

For anyone I've forgotten, and to all I've encountered in this wonderful world, God bless you. Thank you for contributing so richly to my life.

I couldn't have done this without my husband. Love and laughter forever, Honey. My biggest thanks are reserved for the Spirit. Thank you God, for helping me bring this to fruition, and always having my back.

About the Author

This book, *Confessions: Stories to Rock Your Soul* was chosen "Best Unpublished Manuscript" by the Hollywood Book Festival, November 2020.

Nadine Condon is also the author of *Hot Hits Cheap Demos (The Real World-Guide to Music Business Success)*, published by Backbeat Books in 2004.

She lives in the Sonoma Valley in Northern California with her husband, and two rescue cats, Bret and Bart.

Kindly support the following not-for-profit charities: Michael J. Fox Foundation, Angelman Syndrome Foundation, Doctors Without Borders, Mission Hospice and Home Care of San Mateo County, Hospice of the Valley in Phoenix, Arizona, Hope for Paws Animal Rescue in Los Angeles, Sonoma County Acts of Kindness, Catholic Charities of Sonoma County, St. Vincent De Paul of Sonoma County, Old Friends Thoroughbred Retirement Farms, or your local food bank.

Go to NadineCondon.com for more stories and pictures relating to this book, or to contact her.

Made in the USA
Monee, IL
05 June 2022